I0605943

THIS JOURNAL
BELONGS TO

....

THE 100-DAY DEVOTIONAL JOURNAL *for Women*

DONNA K. MALTESE

Print ISBN 979-8-89151-065-4

Cover Image: Greg Jackson, Thinkpen Design

Published by Barbour Publishing, Inc., 1810 Barbour Drive, Uhrichsville, Ohio 44683, www.barbourbooks.com

Our mission is to inspire the world with the life-changing message of the Bible.

Printed in China.

INTRODUCTION

The Lord answered her, "Martha, Martha, you are worried and upset about many things, but one thing is necessary. Mary has made the right choice, and it will not be taken away from her."

LUKE 10:41–42 HCSB

In this life it seems as if we women have a million and one things to do each day. There are households to run, kids to cart, groceries to get, husbands to feed, employers to please, not to mention all our responsibilities in church and the community. Some days we find ourselves staying up into the wee hours of the morning in an effort to check off everything on our to-do lists. It's no wonder we're a bit frazzled and whiny like Martha. We've allowed ourselves to be tempted to accomplish so many of our to-dos that we forget to simply be.

When the busyness of our lives crowds out Christ and our to-do lists squeeze out any time we've penciled in for reading and heeding His Word, it's time to do less and be more. Our hope is that this book may be your springboard for getting into, understanding, and giving yourself up to the guidance of Christ and His Word, for being with Him, sitting at His feet, and absorbing His light.

Day 1

A DETERMINED WOMAN

Where you die, I will die, and there I will be buried. May Yahweh punish me, and do so severely, if anything but death separates you and me.
RUTH 1:17 HCSB

Ruth was one determined woman.

Her story begins with an account of another woman, Naomi. Naomi, her husband Elimelech, and their two sons (Mahlon and Chilion) had left Judah because of a famine in Bethlehem. They settled in Moab. There, at some point, Naomi's husband died. Then her sons married two Moabite women, Orpah and Ruth. Ten years later, both of Naomi's sons died, leaving all three women not only widowed but childless.

Bereft and bitter, Naomi decided to leave the land of her sorrows and head back to Bethlehem. Both daughters-in-law began to follow her. But Naomi told them to go home, back to the house of their mothers. She prayed that God would be kind to them, showing them the love that they'd given her. She prayed they'd find new husbands and be secure once again.

So Orpah turned around and headed home. But Ruth promised Naomi that she would stick to her like glue. And her actions show she was true to her word. By the end of the Bible book that bears her name, Ruth had married a kind and prosperous man, provided a home for Naomi, and given birth to Boaz, who would eventually become the grandfather of David, an ancestor of Jesus.

Sometimes life can seem like one grief piled upon another. It's then we have two choices. We can let that grief take us down and lead us into darkness. Or we can turn it around, get closer to God, and find the determination to keep going, to keep doing, to keep being. Doing so may mean becoming separated from our people and going to a foreign land. Yet, with God by our side, we can be assured of a happy ending and a place of security, and we can become a blessing to those in our present lives and those who will become part of our future.

Lord, make me a woman determined to step out in faith, to go where You lead, to do what You would have me do. Grant me the courage to take that first step in living out Your purpose for my life. In Jesus' name I pray. Amen.

Day 2

QUICKENED BY THE WORD

Remember the word unto thy servant, upon which thou hast caused me to hope. This is my comfort in my affliction: for thy word hath quickened me.
PSALM 119:49–50 KJV

Although the King James Bible is considered one of the greatest masterpieces of English prose, it contains some archaic language in its verses, words we no longer use or can define. One such word is *quicken*.

Strong's Exhaustive Concordance of the Bible tells us that in the verses above, *quicken* is translated from the Hebrew word *haya*, which means "to live, whether literally or figuratively; causatively to revive: keep alive, leave alive, make alive. . .give life, promise life. . .nourish, preserve. . .repair, restore. . .revive, save."

To look at today's verses in simpler terms, we can open *The Message*, which puts Psalm 119:49–50 this way: "Remember what you said to me, your servant—I hang on to these words for dear life! These words hold me up in bad times; yes, your promises rejuvenate me."

In each version, the message is the same. God has made promises to you, His servant. Those promises can lead you to hope. For whatever God says in His Word can provide you with security, comfort, peace, and renewal. To know this is to have a superpower at your fingertips. His promises give you. . .

- **Hope:** "Whatsoever things were written aforetime were written for our learning, that we through patience and comfort of the scriptures might have hope" (Romans 15:4 KJV).
- **Comfort:** "You are close beside me. Your rod and your staff protect and comfort me" (Psalm 23:4 NLT).

- **Rest:** "Come unto me, all ye that labour and are heavy laden, and I will give you rest" (Matthew 11:28 KJV).
- **Peace:** "You will keep in perfect peace all who trust in you, all whose thoughts are fixed on you!" (Isaiah 26:3 NLT).
- **Strength and courage:** "Haven't I commanded you: be strong and courageous? Do not be afraid or discouraged, for the LORD your God is with you wherever you go" (Joshua 1:9 HCSB).
- **Calm:** "He got up and rebuked the wind and the raging waves. So they ceased, and there was a calm" (Luke 8:24 HCSB).
- **Provision:** "My God will supply all your needs according to His riches in glory in Christ Jesus" (Philippians 4:19 HCSB).

No matter what you require, God has the supply just waiting for you in His Word. Seek your answers, nourishment, support, help, and revival there.

Thank You, Lord, for Your Word. Today, I ask that You would revive me in the area of. . .

Day 3

ANYONE, EVERYONE, SOMEONE

A woman who had suffered from a flow of blood for twelve years and had spent all her living upon physicians, and could not be healed by anyone, came up behind Him and touched the fringe of His garment, and immediately her flow of blood ceased.
LUKE 8:43–44 AMPC

How many times have you looked for relief for a condition—whether financial, emotional, mental, spiritual, or physical—but received no help from anyone? And, in the process, felt like a no one?

That's what was happening to this woman with an issue of blood. She'd gone to different doctors for a period of twelve years and "could not be healed by *anyone*" (Luke 8:43 AMPC, emphasis added). Now, having spent all her money on these useless "healers," she decided to reach out to the man named Jesus, the one she'd heard so much about.

This nameless woman had one last chance to be made whole. And she took it. She came up behind Jesus and touched the fringe of His clothing. In doing so, she knew her blood flow ceased at that very instant.

Jesus responded immediately. He knew someone had touched Him. He asked who'd done it. The only answers He got were from His disciples, who said that in this crowd it could have been anyone.

But Jesus repeated His question, saying, "Someone *did* touch Me; for I perceived that [healing] power has gone forth from Me" (verse 46 AMPC, emphasis added).

Realizing she'd been noticed, the woman fell down at Jesus' feet. She told Him why she'd done what she had, then how she'd been immediately cured. To this Jesus replied, "Daughter, your faith (your confidence and trust in Me) has made you well! Go (enter) into peace (untroubled, undisturbed well-being)" (verse 48 AMPC).

Every one of us can see ourselves in this story. We too have looked for healing in other places, from anyone and everyone, then turned to Jesus as a last resort, when in fact it should have been the other way around. Jesus should always be the first one whose shoulder we cry on, the first one to whom we pour out our hearts as we seek healing and strength.

The beauty of seeking Jesus' help is that even though we may think we are really no one special, we'll find that to Jesus we're definitely someone. For He sees each of us as individuals, precious in His sight. And in His care for us, He makes clear that it's our faith and confidence in Him that will make us well, peace filled, and whole.

....

....

....

....

....

....

....

....

....

....

....

....

Lord, may You be the first one I seek when there's trouble. For You alone can make me whole.

Day 4

HELLO, PEACE!

Pray for the peace of Jerusalem: they shall prosper that love thee. Peace be within thy walls, and prosperity within thy palaces. . . . Peace be within thee. Because of the house of the Lord *our God I will seek thy good.*
PSALM 122:6–9 KJV

Today's psalm was one pilgrims sang as they were heading up to Jerusalem. Its writing is attributed to David, the king and the ancestor of our Lord and King, Jesus Christ.

David tells those ascending to the temple that they are to pray for the peace of Jerusalem. He tells the God followers to pray that there would be peace and prosperity not just within the walls of Jerusalem but within its people. For peace within means they will strive for peace together as they travel to the house of the Lord.

This prayer, "Peace be within thee," later became not just a blessing but a greeting, first appearing in 1 Samuel 25 when David and his men were in the wilderness. He'd told ten men to go to Nabal and "greet him in my name; and salute him thus: Peace be to you and to your house and to all that you have" (1 Samuel 25:5–6 AMPC).

Thousands of years later, as part of His instructions to seventy-two disciples who were to go out in pairs to other towns and villages, Jesus said, "Whatever house you enter, first say, Peace be to this household! [Freedom from all the distresses that result from sin be with this family]. And if anyone [worthy] of peace and blessedness is there, the peace and blessedness you wish shall come upon him" (Luke 10:5–6 AMPC).

Jesus Himself used this greeting of peace when He, in postresurrection form, visited His followers. They were all cowering together, "meeting behind locked doors because they were afraid of the Jewish leaders. Suddenly, Jesus was standing there among them! 'Peace be with you,' he said" (John 20:19 NLT).

And as Jesus said that, He showed them the wounds in His hands and side. They were filled with joy and most likely relief that He was among them once again. Then again He said, "Peace be with you" (John 20:21 NLT).

How about you? What fears do you have, fears that have seemingly locked you away from peace? Whatever they are, know that they cannot keep Jesus from coming to you and bringing you the peace of His presence. For once you are rejoined with Him, the relief you experience will be palpable. In His presence, you will be open to receive and experience the perfect peace only He provides.

....

....

....

....

....

....

....

....

....

....

....

....

Lord, here I am. Help me to feel Your presence. Fill me with Your perfect peace.

Day 5

ONLY BELIEVE

Jesus, on hearing this, answered him, Do not be seized with alarm or struck with fear; simply believe [in Me as able to do this], and she shall be made well.
LUKE 8:50 AMPC

In what situations in your life is your faith in Jesus and His abilities lacking? What are you not trusting Him for?

Jairus, a synagogue leader, fell down at Jesus' feet, pleading with Him to come to his house, for there his daughter was dying. As Jesus, apparently wordlessly, began following the man to his home, the woman with the issue of blood reached out and touched Jesus' hem (see Day 3's reading). In other words, the Master was interrupted. And Jairus' situation was temporarily on hold.

Imagine Jairus' reaction. Imagine his frustration, impatience, and possible anger that Jesus had stopped heading to his house where his daughter lay at death's door. What if that had been you? Would you have given up in disgust and just sprinted back home? Would you have tugged on Jesus' robe and said, "Jesus, could You hurry this up? My problem is way more tragic than this woman's—can't You have this conversation with her later?"

Yet we hear nothing of what Jairus may have been thinking or doing. All we know is that while Jesus was speaking with the woman with the issue of blood, "someone came from the synagogue leader's house, saying, 'Your daughter is dead. Don't bother the Teacher anymore' " (Luke 8:49 HCSB).

Overhearing these remarks, Jesus said to Jairus, "Don't be afraid. Only believe, and she will be made well" (verse 50 HCSB). And she was (verses

54–56), to the joy of her parents.

It's faith that will move mountains and overcome obstacles. It's faith that brought down the walls of Jericho. Imagine God telling you to walk around a city with a heavily fortified wall once a day for six days. Finally, on the seventh day, you're to walk around the wall seven times while the priests blow on some trumpets, and then you and all the people are to shout. "Then the city wall will collapse, and the people will advance, each man straight ahead" (Joshua 6:5 HCSB).

The Israelites took God at His word. They believed. And the walls of Jericho came tumbling down! God moved His people forward into the plan He had prepared for them. But He could not do so unless they believed!

Today, consider those areas in your life in which you need only to believe. Remember that your God can do the impossible—when your faith is combined with His power and promises.

Lord, help me only to believe!

Day 6

THE POWER OF RETREAT

Come away by yourselves to a deserted place, and rest a while—for many were [continually] coming and going, and they had not even leisure enough to eat. And they went away in a boat to a solitary place by themselves.

MARK 6:31–32 AMPC

Women often find it difficult to rest, to retreat from the frantic pace of life, to find some time for themselves. Why? Because there's always something that needs to be done. And at times, we firmly believe we're the only ones who'll do that "something" right.

Thus, when we have a spare moment, instead of taking some time for ourselves, we might finally organize that closet or donate those books or write that letter we've been meaning to send to an old friend. Rarely do we use "spare moments" to spend quiet time with God. To retreat into His presence. To rest in His arms.

There's only so much time we can spend living like Martha. Sometimes, perhaps more often than not, we need to become more like Mary. For although it's good to be doing—serving our family, community, church, place of employment, and so on—many times it's better to just be.

Jesus Himself knew the value of retreating from the crowds and spending time alone with God. In Mark 1:35 (KJV) we read, "In the morning, rising up a great while before day, he went out, and departed into a solitary place, and there prayed." Jesus rose, went out, departed, and prayed. That's how determined He was to find some quiet time with God. And it's good Jesus went out early. For just like young children who continually seek out their mommy—all the way to the bathroom—the Lord's disciples went looking for Him. When they eventually found Jesus, they didn't apologize for interrupting His quiet time with His Father but admonished Him, saying, "Everyone's looking for You!" (Mark 1:37 HCSB).

That's when Jesus intimated that the reason He'd headed out to spend quality time with Abba was so He could have the power, the strength, to head into the next town and do what God had called Him to do there: preach.

You too need to retreat into Him. Jesus knows how busy you are, how hard it is for you to find those moments to escape to Him. But He also knows the value of such time alone with Abba God, and the power and peace it gifts you.

Lord, help me to find a place and a time to spend some moments alone with You. Show me the power of retreat.

Day 7

JESUS' CHALLENGE

"You're familiar with the old written law, 'Love your friend,' and its unwritten companion, 'Hate your enemy.' I'm challenging that. I'm telling you to love your enemies. Let them bring out the best in you, not the worst. When someone gives you a hard time, respond with the supple moves of prayer, for then you are working out of your true selves, your God-created selves. This is what God does."
MATTHEW 5:43–45 MSG

This spiritual law of loving our enemies seems to go against our natural inclination. When we're struck, we often want to strike back, verbally if not physically. Yet Jesus tells us to take a different tack. To love those who hurt us, no matter how hard it is for us to do so.

Yet that's not all! Jesus first reminds us of the law that said the punishment must match the injury inflicted upon us. In other words, we're to take "an eye for an eye and a tooth for a tooth" (Matthew 5:38 HCSB). Then He tells us that we're not to resist someone who does us evil. In fact, we're to do the opposite! If someone slaps us on the right cheek, we're then to offer up our left cheek to his hand. If someone takes our shirt, we're to give that person our coat as well. If we're forced to go one mile, we're to go two. (See Matthew 5:38–42.)

All these actions we're to take when dealing with people who seem to be taking advantage of us may be hard to acclimate to. They are so counterintuitive to our flesh. Yet Jesus commands us to live and move in the Spirit. To follow Him. The one who suffered and died at the hand of His enemies so that we could be saved. So that we could have a relationship with God Almighty.

If anyone deserves to hold a grudge against those who wished Him harm as well as those who actually harmed Him, it's Jesus. Yet He was also the one who moved in love on the night He was arrested. When Jesus' disciples realized what was about to happen, "one of them struck the high priest's slave and cut off his right ear. But Jesus responded, 'No more of this!' And touching his ear, He healed him" (Luke 22:50–51 HCSB).

Loving those who hate or hurt us is a big ask. But it is doable—when you ask for Jesus' help. It's the only way to truly live!

Lord, help me to love those who don't love me. Give me the power and the passion to turn the other cheek, loving as You loved, living as You lived. Amen.

Day 8

HELP IS ON THE WAY

I lift my eyes toward the mountains. Where will my help come from?
My help comes from the Lord, the Maker of heaven and earth.
He will not allow your foot to slip; your Protector will not slumber.
Indeed, the Protector of Israel does not slumber or sleep.
Psalm 121:1–4 HCSB

When wave after wave after wave of alarming and generally bad news continually knocks you down, it becomes more and more difficult to get back up on your feet, to steel yourself against the next onslaught that may come from who knows where.

Fortunately, people of God have a place they can go to calm their nerves, to clear their minds of all the what-ifs swirling inside, weighing them down, distracting them from walking the pathway God has laid out for them.

Psalm 121 tells us that our help comes from God. That we need to lift our eyes up to Him, the one who will not allow life to trip us up. The 24-7 protector who never sleeps but continuously has His eyes upon us and His ears attuned to our voices.

God is our constant guardian. His constant presence shields us from the sun during the day and the glow of the moon at night. He promises to keep us from all evil. To protect our lives, keeping us safe as we go out and as we come in. (See Psalm 121:5–8.)

In Psalm 20 we're reminded that God will not only protect us from trouble but send us help and sustain us. We who look to Him for help are not like those who trust in material machines for strength, power, and protection. For those things don't have the same power as our Lord. No, we trust in the name of God alone, the supernatural powerhouse who is known as Yahweh, provider, protector, the all-powerful Lord of lords and King of kings.

When the world gets you down, when the news is more than you can take, when you need help, know that God has His eyes on you. His ears are open to your call. He, who created you, knows all about what you have experienced, what you now face. He already knows what's going to happen. He knows the beginning and the end. He knows His plans for you.

So don't allow anything or anyone to drag you down. Just simply lift your eyes and spirit up to God. Keep your focus on Him. He's got you.

Thank You, Lord, for taking such good care of me. For constantly watching over me. For helping me make my way through this world. For keeping me safe in the palm of Your hand.

Day 9

GOD, THE PROVIDER

The Lord is my shepherd; I have all that I need. He lets me rest in green meadows; he leads me beside peaceful streams. He renews my strength. He guides me along right paths, bringing honor to his name.
Psalm 23:1–3 NLT

We live in a world where the rich are getting richer, and the poor poorer. These days it seems harder than ever to make ends meet. It's no wonder people are stressed about finances, losing precious sleep at night, wondering how long they'll be able to survive living paycheck to paycheck.

Yet believers have a never-ending resource—the Lord God, our Good Shepherd. He's the one who promises to provide all we need. He's the one who gives us the rest we require, who guides us into the peace and calm we crave, and who renews our strength as He leads us in the right direction.

The apostle Paul confirms this idea of God supplying all our needs (Philippians 4:19). He tells us not to be anxious, knowing our supplier is always looking out for us, putting in our paths today what we will need tomorrow. Thus, we are to "be careful for nothing; but in every thing by prayer and supplication with thanksgiving let [our] requests be made known unto God" (verse 6 KJV). When we live our lives this way, when we refuse to be anxious over money today and possible needs tomorrow, when we take our cares to God, laying all our needs before Him and thanking Him for what He has already given us, we'll find not just the provisions we require but the peace that comes with knowing He'll answer our prayers (verse 7).

When the Jews were wandering in the wilderness, God provided them with a type of food they'd never seen nor tasted before. The people called it manna (meaning "What is it?"). The Israelites were told to gather only what was needed for the day. Then, on the sixth day, they were to gather twice as much as usual so that on the Sabbath they could rest from gathering this "angel food" (Exodus 16:4–5).

Just as God provided for those wandering in the desert, He'll provide for you. He's the answer to and supplier of all your needs. Rest in that knowledge. Be anxious for nothing. Your God will take care of you.

I praise and thank You, God, my provider,
for what You have already supplied me.
I entrust all I have and am to You,
knowing that because of You, I do
not and will not lack. Amen.

Day 10

THE GOD WHO SEES YOU

She called the name of the Lord Who spoke to her, You are a God of seeing, for she said, Have I [not] even here [in the wilderness] looked upon Him Who sees me [and lived]? Or have I here also seen [the future purposes or designs of] Him Who sees me? Therefore the well was called Beer-lahai-roi [A well to the Living One Who sees me].
GENESIS 16:13–14 AMPC

Ever felt invisible? That no one around you sees what's happening in your life or understands what you are going through? That no one is acknowledging (or ever has acknowledged) your feelings?

Meet Hagar. An Egyptian. She was Sarai's maid. When Sarai got impatient for God's promised child to materialize, she decided maybe she could get a child by giving Hagar to Abraham as a surrogate. Abraham went along with the arrangement. Soon Hagar became pregnant. Sarai hated her for it, so she began to mistreat Hagar.

The only recourse Hagar saw open to her was to run away. So that's what she did. Before long, the angel of the Lord found her by a well of water in the wilderness. He asked her, "Hagar, slave of Sarai, where have you come from and where are you going?" (Genesis 16:8 HCSB).

Hagar told him she was running away from Sarai. That's when the angel of the Lord told her she had to go back. To put up with Sarai's abuse. And that God would give her (Hagar) more descendants than she could count. So Hagar named that well Beer-lahai-roi, "A well to the Living One Who Sees Me."

The God who saw Hagar sees you. Not only does He see you, but He knows your name. He knows your situation. He knows exactly what will happen, has happened, and is happening in your life.

So on those days when you feel invisible, misunderstood, ignored, downtrodden, don't run away, but run to the God who sees you. Know that He has a purpose for you, a plan for your life. He has created you for a special role in this world. And no matter how hard that path may seem, He will be with you every step of the way, watching over you, looking after you.

Dear God who sees me, when I'm wandering in the wilderness, I pray You would help me find my way, even if it means going back from whence I came. Thank You for watching over me, for seeing me, for loving me. Amen.

Day 11

COURSE STEERING 101

Inquire first, I pray you, for the word of the Lord today. . . .
The person of understanding will acquire skill and attain to sound counsel [so that he may be able to steer his course rightly].
1 KINGS 22:5; PROVERBS 1:5 AMPC

You have a major decision to make regarding your finances, career, calling, church life, family, or a certain relationship. A decision that will affect not only you but the lives of those around you. So you determine to get advice from people who may have more wisdom than you. Chances are you'll intentionally or unintentionally ask the advice of someone who'll tell you the answer you want to hear.

That's what happened when King Ahab of Israel was trying to persuade King Jehoshaphat of Judah to battle with him against Ramoth-gilead. Ahab asked the opinion of certain advisors—more sycophants than prophets—who he knew would say what he wanted them to say, namely, "Yes! That's a great idea! Of course God will bring you victory!" (see 1 Kings 22:5–7).

Jehoshaphat, not yet convinced, asked Ahab if there was any other prophet of God whom they could ask. Only one, said Ahab. "Micaiah. . .by whom we may inquire of the Lord, but I hate him, for he never prophesies good for me, but evil" (1 Kings 22:8 AMPC). Yet on Micaiah they called. And he, of course, predicted not just death but disaster for Ahab. His exact words were "I saw all Israel scattered upon the hills as sheep that have no shepherd, and the Lord said, These have no master. Let them return every man to his house in peace" (verse 17 AMPC).

Ahab commanded Micaiah to be put in prison and fed "only bread and water until I come back safely" (verse 27 HCSB). But Ahab never did come back. During the attack on Ramoth-gilead, an enemy arrow struck Ahab through the joints of his armor. He bled out as the battle raged on. "He died that evening, and blood from his wound flowed into the bottom of the chariot. Then the cry rang out in the army as the sun set, declaring: Each man to his own city, and each man to his own land!" (verses 35–36 HCSB). All, even down to the detail of Ahab's blood being licked up by dogs, happened "according to the word of the LORD that He had spoken" (verse 38 HCSB).

The moral? When you need advice, first apply to God. Then ask someone who you know will give you good advice so that you can steer your course rightly.

Lord, I need some advice. . . .

Day 12

STILLNESS

Let be and be still, and know (recognize and understand) that I am God.
PSALM 46:10 AMPC

The word *still* in today's verse comes from the Hebrew word *rapa*, which means "to let alone, let go, be slack, be still." And that's what God wants you to do. To not be anxious about anything. To remember that He is in charge—He has the answer to whatever problem or situation is causing you to lose sleep.

To be able to obey this command of God, to reach the state where you can be still, to get to the place where you put whatever is against you into His hands and leave all up to Him, you need to know who the "I am God" is.

Psalm 46:1 tells us God is our refuge, our strength. He's mighty. A helper who is always found when trouble arises. Because He's on our side, residing within and without, we need not fear even "though the earth should change and though the mountains be shaken into the midst of the seas, though its waters roar and foam, though the mountains tremble at its swelling and tumult" (verses 2–3 AMPC).

This amazing God, Lord of all creation, who is always with us, is our "Refuge (our Fortress and High Tower)" (verse 7 AMPC). He is the one to whom we can run.

We're also to remember all He has done. When the Israelites were seemingly trapped between the Egyptian army and the Red Sea, Moses told them, "Fear not; stand still (firm, confident, undismayed) and see the salvation of the Lord which He will work for you today. For the Egyptians you have seen today you shall never see again. The Lord will fight for you, and you shall hold your peace and remain at rest" (Exodus 14:13–14 AMPC). And He did!

The God who divided the Red Sea so His people could walk through on dry ground is the same God who resides in you today. He's the same God who commands you to be free from anxiety and worry. To leave all that you are, have, and love in His hands.

Today, remember who you are and who God is. Remember your respective roles. You are to be still, to leave all in His hands and allow Him to be your refuge, tower, and stronghold (Psalm 46:11 AMPC).

....

....

....

....

....

....

....

....

....

....

....

....

....

....

It is so hard for me to be still sometimes, Lord. Yet I know that's what You call me to do. So help me to know You more, trust You more, believe You more, feel Your presence more. Help me begin today to be still—in You.

Day 13

BETWEEN HEAVEN AND EARTH

"Look, I am with you and will watch over you wherever you go. I will bring you back to this land, for I will not leave you until I have done what I have promised you." When Jacob awoke from his sleep, he said, "Surely the LORD is in this place, and I did not know it." He was afraid and said, "What an awesome place this is! This is none other than the house of God. This is the gate of heaven."
GENESIS 28:15–17 HCSB

Jacob was on the run. He'd earlier tricked his brother, Esau, into turning over all the rights of the firstborn. Then, at his mother Rebekah's urging, he'd stolen Esau's blessing from their father, Isaac.

Esau was so filled with hate and anger that he said, "I will soon be mourning my father's death. Then I will kill my brother, Jacob" (Genesis 27:41 NLT).

Overhearing Esau's threat, Rebekah told Jacob to run away to her brother Laban in Haran. She figured her favorite son could stay there until Esau cooled off. And while Jacob was there, he might as well find a wife.

So Jacob ran off, never to see his mother alive again. On his way to Haran, Jacob stopped in the wilderness at sundown. There he slept, using a stone for a pillow, and dreamed of a stairway that extended from earth to heaven. God's angels were going up and down on it.

God stood at the top of the stairway and introduced Himself to Jacob. He told him that the ground he was sleeping on belonged to him and his descendants, who would "be as numerous as the dust of the earth!" (Genesis 28:14 NLT). He assured Jacob that He'd be with him always, that He would not leave him until His promises had been realized.

About this scene F. B. Meyer writes:

> *There is an open way between Heaven and earth for each of us. The movement of the tide and circulation of the blood are not more regular than the intercommunication between Heaven and earth. Jacob may have thought that God was local; now he found him to be omnipresent. Every lonely spot was his house, filled with angels.*[1]

No matter what you're running from or to, no matter how far away from home you may roam, no matter where you go, God is already there. Be assured that He is and always will be with you, waiting to hold you, advise you, encourage you, and love you.

Lord, thank You so much for being wherever I need You. Help me to be more aware of Your presence every day.

1 F. B. Meyer, *Through the Bible Day by Day: A Devotional Commentary*, https://www.studylight.org/commentaries/eng/fbm/genesis-28.html.

Day 14

GETTING STRAIGHT

There was a woman there who for eighteen years had had an infirmity caused by a spirit (a demon of sickness). She was bent completely forward and utterly unable to straighten herself up or to look upward. And when Jesus saw her, He called [her to Him] and said to her, Woman, you are released from your infirmity! Then He laid [His] hands on her, and instantly she was made straight.

LUKE 13:11–13 AMPC

There are times in life when some trouble or another has us bent over. Our eyes, now fixed on our feet, have difficulty taking in everything around us. Yet still, no matter how long we suffer, we continue to seek out God, to worship Him, to find solace in His house, to bring ourselves into His presence. For we realize that, in regard to some situations and circumstances, there is little we can do to help ourselves, to straighten ourselves out.

Such was the situation in which this woman found herself. For eighteen years she had been bent over, "utterly unable to straighten herself up or to look upward."

Then comes Jesus. In His immense love and compassion for people, He sees her and calls her over to Him. He speaks, addressing her directly. He commands her healing. Then He touches her. With faith and trust melded with and amplified by Jesus' power, the bent-over woman is instantaneously made straight! For the first time in eighteen years, she could look up. And what did she see? Jesus' face!

No wonder the woman erupted in praises to God. Can't you just see her leaping up in the air, clapping her hands, grinning from ear to ear?

Perhaps in some way you too are bound. Perhaps worry and anxiety are working to keep you bowed down. Perhaps you've been afflicted by something for so long that you have little hope of ever being released from it.

When we are afflicted and cannot help or remedy ourselves, it's time to reach out to the Master Healer, the Shepherd of our souls. It's time to enter His presence. To come to Him, to be taught by Him and touched by Him. And upon hearing His word to us and experiencing His hand upon us, to find our freedom, to be loosed from whatever is plaguing us. To finally stand up straight and begin praising Him, pouring forth all the joy in our spirit and heart.

You already know, Lord Jesus, what has been keeping me from standing straight. Help me find relief and release now, Lord. In Your name I pray. Amen.

Day 15

THE STRENGTH OF HIS PRESENCE

The LORD turned to him and said, "Go in the strength you have and deliver Israel from the power of Midian. Am I not sending you?" He said to Him, "Please, Lord, how can I deliver Israel? Look, my family is the weakest in Manasseh, and I am the youngest in my father's house." "But I will be with you," the LORD said to him.

JUDGES 6:14–16 HCSB

Sometimes, when we're under pressure, we take to hiding out. We figure that might be the only way to stick it out when we face trouble no matter which way we turn. But God has other ideas.

Such was the case with Gideon. The Midianites kept troubling Israel. They continually made raids into the territory of God's people, destroying their produce, taking their animals, leaving nothing for the Israelites to eat. So the Israelites called out to God for help.

God responded by sending His angel to Ophrah. There He found Gideon "threshing wheat in the wine vat in order to hide it from the Midianites" (Judges 6:11 HCSB). The angel spoke to Gideon, saying, "Mighty hero, the LORD is with you!" (verse 12 NLT).

Gideon responded by asking Him a question (one that may be on many minds these days): "Please Sir, if the LORD is with us, why has all this happened?" (verse 13 HCSB).

That's when God told Gideon to go in the strength he had, because God was sending him. Regardless of how Gideon saw himself, God saw him as a person of valor. And God made it clear that He would give Gideon all the strength he needed to do what God called him to do.

The apostle Paul, in his letter to the Philippian church, made the same point, writing: "I have strength for all things in Christ Who empowers me [I am ready for anything and equal to anything through Him Who infuses inner strength into me]" (Philippians 4:13 AMPC).

God wants you to know that no matter what is happening in your life, no matter what chaos is going on in this world, you will receive all the strength you need in Christ. In Him you can accomplish all He wants you to accomplish.

Women have for centuries been called the weaker sex. But with God, there is no male or female, owner or slave. There's only a person after God's own heart, an individual who seeks to please Him, whose spirit knows that in Him lies all the strength she needs.

Oh God my strength, I seek Your presence today. For with Your power, Your supernatural energy, I can do all You call me to do. Amen.

Day 16

FAR MORE VALUABLE

"That is why I tell you not to worry about everyday life—whether you have enough food and drink, or enough clothes to wear. Isn't life more than food, and your body more than clothing? Look at the birds. They don't plant or harvest or store food in barns, for your heavenly Father feeds them. And aren't you far more valuable to him than they are?"
MATTHEW 6:25–26 NLT

Throughout history, women have been undervalued, sometimes treated as nothing more than property. It has only been over the last one hundred years that women have been able to vote in elections in the United States.

Yet even now we, who are considered by some to be the invisible infrastructure in society, sometimes receive less pay even though we are performing the same work as men. On top of that, we still have many duties in the home to perform, tasks that are not considered true work. Yet we know that taking care of family—from kids to elders—is some of the toughest work there is. It's enough to make a woman—whether she works inside or outside the home—feel undervalued or totally unvalued.

Thank God for Jesus. He treasured women. In fact, He had many women followers, namely, Mary Magdalene, Joanna, Susanna, "and many others, who ministered to and provided for Him and [the disciples] out of their property and personal belongings" (Luke 8:3 AMPC).

Women not only supported Jesus financially but remained with Him when His disciples deserted Him. Along with Mary (mother of Jesus), Mary (mother of James and Joses/Joseph), and Salome (mother of James and John), Mary Magdalene not only was a witness to Jesus' crucifixion and burial (Matthew 27:61; 28:1; Mark 15:40, 47; John 19:25) and among the women who went to the tomb the day after the Sabbath (Mark 16:1; John 20:1), but was the first to see Him alive after His resurrection (Mark 16:9)! And she was the first evangelist, for it was Mary Magdalene who went to tell others she'd seen the risen Christ (Luke 24:10; John 20:18)!

The point is, Jesus valued women. Now we must realize we're also valuable to our heavenly Father. Doing so will keep us from worrying. For when we understand how much God appreciates us, how worthy He believes our work to be, we'll become more certain that He will fully provide for us—physically, emotionally, and spiritually.

Assure me, Lord, that I am a being of value in Your eyes. And because You consider me worthy of Your love and care, I need not worry. In Jesus' name. Amen.

Day 17

FIRMLY GRIPPED

"Don't panic. I'm with you. There's no need to fear for I'm your God. I'll give you strength. I'll help you. I'll hold you steady, keep a firm grip on you. . . . I, your God, have a firm grip on you and I'm not letting go. I'm telling you, 'Don't panic. I'm right here to help you.'"
Isaiah 41:10, 13 MSG

When our children were little, chances are we were their main protector. When it came to crossing a street, we made sure we had a very firm grip on their little hands. We were their defender, their place of safety. In their eyes, we were the pillar of security they clung to.

And God is the same for us. Because He is with us, reaching out with His huge hand and holding us tight to His side, we are safe. Because of God in our life, standing between us and the unknown, the light that permeates the darkness, and because He has promised that He will never let us go and that no matter what happens He will be with us, helping us, we need not fear anything.

When we feel helpless, we need not despair. For we have a connection to the supernatural, almighty helper who created us and the world in which we live! The one who holds us by His right hand, keeping a firm grip on us, is the same one who said:

> *"When you're in over your head, I'll be there with you. When you're in rough waters, you will not go down. When you're between a rock and a hard place, it won't be a dead end—because I am God, your personal God, the Holy of Israel, your Savior. I paid a huge price for you: all of Egypt, with rich Cush and Seba thrown in! That's how much you*

mean to me! That's how much I love you! I'd sell off the whole world to get you back, trade the creation just for you." (Isaiah 43:2–4 MSG)

This is the promise God has made you. All you need to do is believe it.

If you're not yet there, make a concentrated effort to get there. Every day, read over today's verses. Do so until you believe God is present with you all the time. Until you know He has a firm and eternal grip on you, one He will not release. That He will be there—right there—to help you whenever you need it. That He will pull you out of whatever trouble you find yourself in.

God's got you.

....

....

....

....

....

....

....

....

....

....

....

....

....

....

Thank You, Lord, for forever looking out for me. Help me believe You will never let me go!

Day 18

THE POWER OF THE SECRET PLACE

He who dwells in the secret place of the Most High shall remain stable and fixed under the shadow of the Almighty [Whose power no foe can withstand]. I will say of the Lord, He is my Refuge and my Fortress, my God; on Him I lean and rely, and in Him I [confidently] trust!
PSALM 91:1–2 AMPC

There are certain verses from the Bible that you'll forever find in devotional books. And today's are most likely on the top of that list. Why? Because they're powerful. They're verses we need to engrave on our hearts and minds.

Psalm 91 informs us that the person who rests in God, making Him her refuge, abiding in that secret place, trusting in and relying on Him alone, will find the stability she longs for. For her location is fixed beneath the wings of the Almighty—the one "whose power no foe can withstand"!

When you're living a life devoted to God, existing in close fellowship with Him, making Him your refuge and fortress, so many blessings are available to you: He'll rescue you from the hunter's net and a destructive plague; He'll cover you with His wings; His faithfulness to you will be a protective shield.

When you live a life this close to God, you won't fear the terrors that come in the night, nor the arrow that's aiming for you during the day. God promises that those who live in Him will not be harmed. "For He will give His angels orders concerning you, to protect you in all your ways" (Psalm 91:11 HCSB). He promises, "I will rescue those who love me. I will protect those who trust in my name. When they call on me, I will answer; I will be with them in trouble. I will rescue and honor them. I will reward them with a long life and give them my salvation" (verses 14–16 NLT).

Woman of the Way, what are you waiting for?

Today, work your way into that secret place. Find some time to be alone with God in the early hours. Put your day in His hands. Ask Him to keep you sheltered under His wings. Remember that He is greater than any other power—seen and unseen—that may come against you. Keep in mind that living and abiding in His will is the safest place you can be.

Lord, help me find my way into that secret place in You, my refuge, my fortress, my God.

Day 19

THE PRODIGAL DAUGHTER

And when he came to himself, he said, How many hired servants of my father's have bread enough and to spare, and I perish with hunger! . . . And he arose, and came to his father. But when he was yet a great way off, his father saw him, and had compassion, and ran, and fell on his neck, and kissed him.
LUKE 15:17, 20 KJV

To stifle the Pharisees' murmurings about His drawing out and keeping company with sinners, Jesus tells three parables. The first is the parable of the lost sheep (Luke 15:3–7), in which the shepherd who loses one of his one hundred sheep will leave the ninety-nine to go off and look for the lost one. And when he finds it, he will rejoice and celebrate.

The second parable is about the woman with ten coins (verses 8–10). She diligently searches until she finds the lost coin. And when she finds it, she calls all near and dear to her to celebrate with her.

The third parable is about the prodigal son (verses 11–32). Here, the younger of two sons asks his father for his inheritance ahead of time. The father acquiesces to the son, who then leaves home and fritters away his fortune in lascivious living. It's when he's destitute and serving slop to pigs that he comes to himself. He decides to go home, apologize to his dad, and ask for a job as a servant.

His father, obviously looking for his son day after day, sees him approaching from a long way off. Filled with compassion for this lost boy, he runs to him, falls on his neck, and kisses him. Before the son can get his full confession out, the father is demanding a robe, a ring, and some shoes be brought out and put on his son. Then they'll all celebrate the one who was lost and is now found.

God is that Father who is always looking for us to come to our senses and walk back to Him. For when we do, He goes into action. Looking, He sees us, His compassion rising up to the surface. Running, He reaches us. Falling, He holds us. Kissing, He loves us.

Prodigal daughters, if you find yourself drifting apart from God, wanting to go your own way or already living away from Him, come to your senses. God is ready and waiting to welcome you home.

Father God, thank You for loving me more than I deserve. Help me to come to my senses when I begin drifting away. Pull me safely back into Your embrace.

Day 20

ABANDONED TO GOD

I waited and waited and waited for God. At last he looked; finally he listened. He lifted me out of the ditch, pulled me from deep mud. He stood me up on a solid rock to make sure I wouldn't slip. He taught me how to sing the latest God-song, a praise-song to our God. More and more people are seeing this: they enter the mystery, abandoning themselves to God.
Psalm 40:1–3 MSG

God has a specific plan for us. And sometimes we need to be patient as we wait for Him to move in our lives, to answer our prayers, to show us where He would have us go.

It's all about timing. Events happen according to God's schedule, not ours. Yet when He does move, we realize His timing is absolutely perfect.

Our part is to wait on God patiently. And as we wait, to continue to pray. And as we pray, to hope perseveringly until God responds to our prayer and moves to help us. No matter how far we've fallen, how desperate our trouble, how great our calamity, God is able to lift us out of the pit, to pull us out of the mud that refuses to release us.

When God does pull you out of the muck and mire, He'll stand you up on a rock, a place of strength and safety. He'll put you on solid footing, ensuring you don't slip. And then He'll teach you how to sing a song of praise to Him.

When you do these things, when you, a woman of the Way, wait for God patiently, keeping your head and hope up until He responds, showing you will not give up on Him—as He never gives up on you—you'll be an example to other people of what happens when a person joyfully abandons her present and future to God. People will want to have what you have, be as you are, hope as you hope. They'll want to enter the mystery that a relationship with God entails.

Today, examine where you are. Consider what message your attitude is conveying to others. Then, if necessary, apply to God, asking Him to give you the patience you need until He moves on your behalf. And when He does, when He lifts you out, pulls you up onto solid rock, give voice to the song He teaches you.

I pray, Lord, that You would help me enter the mystery of You. That You would show me how to abandon myself to Your will and way. Give me the hope and patience I need today so I may sing an amazing song tomorrow.

Day 21

WHOLE IN FAITH

One of them, when he saw that he was healed, turned back, and with a loud voice glorified God, and fell down on his face at his feet, giving him thanks: and he was a Samaritan. And Jesus answering said, Were there not ten cleansed? but where are the nine? There are not found that returned to give glory to God, save this stranger. And he said unto him, Arise, go thy way: thy faith hath made thee whole.
LUKE 17:15–19 KJV

From the very beginning of your conscious life, you may have felt as if something was missing. You may have thought, *For some reason, I don't feel quite whole.*

And then you met Jesus Christ. Now you know why material possessions don't make you happy—but having Jesus in your life does. For He makes you feel complete.

In Luke 17:11–19, Jesus was traveling to Jerusalem. On the way, He met up with ten lepers. Being unclean, they stood at a distance from Him and yelled out, "Jesus, Master, have mercy on us" (Luke 17:13 KJV).

After looking them over, Jesus instructed them to show themselves to the priests. On their way to do just that, they were cured, proving not only that Jesus does heal but that He can do so from a distance!

Yet only one leper, a Samaritan (a race despised by Jews), having seen that he was healed, walked back to Jesus then fell to the ground at His feet. In a loud voice, he praised God and thanked Jesus.

Jesus wondered aloud where the other nine lepers He'd healed were, why only the foreigner, the Samaritan, came back to praise God and thank Him. Then He said to the renewed man, "Arise, go thy way; thy faith hath made thee whole."

Each one of us has a God-shaped hole within us. Only His presence within us can make us feel complete. And feeling complete is an essential part of our inner happiness. For when we're whole, we need no one else's validation to make us happy and content.

How whole are you in your own faith? In what areas of your life have you neglected to ask for God's mercy? If mercy and healing were given, did you raise your praise to God and give thanks to Jesus?

Why not lift yourself up to the Lord and praise Him today! Allow Him to complete you.

Lord, here I am at Your feet. I praise You for all You have done in and through me. I thank Your Son for who I am and will become. You, my three-in-one God, complete me.

Day 22

A LIGHT THING

You shall not see wind or rain, yet that ravine shall be filled with water, so you, your cattle, and your beasts [of burden] may drink. This is but a light thing in the sight of the Lord. He will deliver the Moabites also into your hands.
2 KINGS 3:17–18 AMPC

One of the things that may keep us from progressing in our walk with God is the limits we put on Him. Sometimes we forget He can do anything and everything. We forget that nothing is impossible with Him. And so we imagine obstacles in our path that keep us from walking forward, from doing what God has called us to do.

The king of Moab rebelled against King Joram of Israel when the latter's father, Ahab, died. So King Joram called his men to war. Then he sent word to King Jehoshaphat, asking if he would go with him against Moab. Jehoshaphat said, "I will go. I am as you are, my people as your people, my horses as your horses" (2 Kings 3:7 HCSB).

After traveling for seven days in the wilderness of Edom, the kings of Israel, Judah, and Edom had used up the water supply for their men and animals. "Then the king of Israel said, Alas! The Lord has called [us] three kings together to be delivered into Moab's hand! But Jehoshaphat said, Is there no prophet of the Lord here by whom we may inquire of the Lord?" (verses 10–11 AMPC).

Then all three kings went to see Elisha. The prophet, who had no kind words to say to King Joram, whose parents had followed false gods, said, "As the LORD of Hosts lives, I stand before Him. If I did not have respect for King Jehoshaphat of Judah, I would not look at you; I wouldn't take notice of you" (verse 14 HCSB). Then Elisha asked for a musician to be brought to him. As the music played, the hand of God came upon the prophet and he told the three kings that God would fill a ravine with water so that their armies and animals could quench their thirst. But that was nothing compared to what else God would do: God said He would give them victory over Moab. And He did.

When you ask God for help, keep in mind that He can do so much more than you could ever think, ask, or imagine (Ephesians 3:20)!

Help me remember, Lord, that with You all things are possible. Help me to increase my faith, to move away from my limited thinking—for with You, there are no limits. There are no obstacles.

Day 23

BY GOD'S LIGHT

By your words I can see where I'm going;
they throw a beam of light on my dark path.
PSALM 119:105 MSG

Life is complicated—but there is hope. For we who believe have the Word to light our path.

When you're full of fear, wondering if you'll have enough money to buy a car, build a house, or retire, look to the Word. When you're tortured by doubt, wondering if you'll make it through your pregnancy or survive the terrible twos or teenage years as your children grow, find assurance in the Word.

The lamp of God has been, is, and forever will be kept burning with the oil of the Holy Spirit. It will help you not only find your path but keep your feet upon it. The Word will give you the confidence to make decisions, put your hope in God, and keep calm.

You know what it's like when you're walking around a dark house, especially one you're not familiar with. You might stumble, stub your toe, or trip over what you cannot see. As you face an unknown future, you'll find that God's Word is the beacon you can follow, the candle in your hand, the glow you need to survive in the darkness of this world.

So bask in the light of God's Word in the dark hours of the early morning each day. Don't venture out into the wilderness of modern society without first seeking the direction you need to keep to God's pathway. Seek that same Word in the evening, seeing it as a night-light that will guide you gently into your slumber. Rest easy knowing that all you need to do is reach out and it will be there, dispelling whatever fears, sorrows, or doubts you may have as you enter the world of dreams.

Be as a little child, faithfully trusting God, certain that He will help you find your way. Having been a child yourself, you know what it means to lose your way, to be separated from your parents and experience that sinking feeling inside. You most likely remember what it was like to be frightened by the darkness, to wonder if the monsters underneath your bed or in your closet would harm you in the deep shadows of the night.

How wonderful that no matter how frightened you may become, you have a bright light within your reach. And as soon as you flick it on, all those doubts, fears, and terrors of darkness immediately dissipate.

Thank You, Lord, for the comforting, guiding light of Your good Word!

Day 24

REALIGNMENT

With God nothing is ever impossible and no word from God shall be without power or impossible of fulfillment. Then Mary said, Behold, I am the handmaiden of the Lord; let it be done to me according to what you have said. And the angel left her.
LUKE 1:37–38 AMPC

When the angel Gabriel first appeared to the girl Mary in Galilee, announcing that she was favored, that the Lord was with her, she was stunned. And perhaps confused. While she was trying to comprehend what she was seeing and hearing, what this angel's greeting might mean, the angel spoke again. In fact, he almost rushed through the information he was so eager to impart to her listening ears, saying:

> *"Don't be afraid, Mary. . .for you have found favor with God! You will conceive and give birth to a son, and you will name him Jesus. He will be very great and will be called the Son of the Most High. The Lord God will give him the throne of his ancestor David. And he will reign over Israel forever; his Kingdom will never end!" (Luke 1:30–33 NLT)*

After taking in these words, Mary asked how this would happen. For although she was betrothed to Joseph, she had never been with a man. Gabriel got further into the details, saying, "The Holy Spirit will come upon you, and the power of the Most High will overshadow you. So the baby to be born will be holy, and he will be called the Son of God" (verse 35 NLT).

Perhaps to convince Mary of the doability of his words, Gabriel added that Mary's elderly cousin Elizabeth herself was pregnant. People had said she was barren, but she had conceived a son and was six months along in her pregnancy! How was this possible? Because God's Word never fails. All His promises will, in their time, become a reality.

Mary accepted the angel's seemingly far-fetched proposal by describing herself as God's willing servant and adding a prayer that all the angel pronounced would become her reality.

The angel's announcement had turned upside down whatever Mary might have planned for herself and Joseph. In this short conversation with God's angel, Mary's desires were redirected to align with God's words.

If you live a life in which your desires are aligned with God's will, if you live your life believing His promises are part of your reality, if you proclaim yourself to be God's servant, open to whatever He may suggest, you too may become a witness to and a participant in the impossible.

Lord, please align my desires to match Your will and promises.

Day 25

BLESSED IN BELIEVING

"How could this happen to me, that the mother of my Lord should come to me? For you see, when the sound of your greeting reached my ears, the baby leaped for joy inside me! She who has believed is blessed because what was spoken to her by the Lord will be fulfilled!"
LUKE 1:43–45 HCSB

Two humble, godly women meet. They are relatives, cousins. One elderly, the other very young. Both are undergoing miraculous experiences: they are pregnant—a miracle in itself! The elder, Elizabeth, is carrying the one who would be "filled with the Holy Spirit while still in his mother's womb," a prophet having "the spirit and power of Elijah" (Luke 1:15, 17 HCSB). The younger, Mary, is carrying within her the Son of God who would save her people (verses 32–35).

These women's minds are not only on their daily humdrum chores and duties but also on the plans God has established for their children, from their inception to their adulthood. As soon as Elizabeth sets her eyes on Mary, she and her unborn child are moved by the Holy Spirit to celebrate the privilege of meeting the mother of their Lord and Savior. Even more striking is when Elizabeth pronounces Mary as blessed because she has believed that what God has told her, the promises He has made through the angel Gabriel, will indeed be fulfilled.

Here, Elizabeth may have been thinking about her husband, Zechariah, who had expressed doubt when the angel Gabriel told him his wife would bear a son (verses 13–23). For instead of being blessed in believing, Zechariah had been struck dumb for his doubt.

From these accounts it appears that faith is the foundation of true fulfillment and joy. Because of her faith, Mary believed that what God had said would become her reality. Because of her belief, she received the fulfillment of His promises. And because part of God's promise had already been presented to her in the flesh (Elizabeth's pregnancy), Mary couldn't help but sing a song of praise to her Lord.

How would your life change if you believed that what God promised would be fulfilled? What would your day-to-day existence look like if you were convinced that the God who gave you His promises would see them to fruition? How often would you stop during the day to praise God for the promises He is fulfilling in your life and the lives of others?

Lord, give me a faith that sees Your promises as my reality so that I might be blessed in believing!

Day 26

THE LITTLE MAID AND THE MIGHTY MAN: PART 1

Naaman, commander of the army of the king of Syria, was a great man with his master, accepted [and acceptable], because by him the Lord had given victory to Syria. He was also a mighty man of valor, but he was a leper. The Syrians had gone out in bands and had brought away captive out of the land of Israel a little maid, and she waited on Naaman's wife. She said to her mistress, Would that my lord were with the prophet who is in Samaria! For he would heal him of his leprosy.

2 KINGS 5:1–3 AMPC

Ninety-three women speak in the Bible. Of those ninety-three women, forty-nine are named. The actual number of words spoken by these women (in the Revised Standard Version) comes to 14,056 words, about 1.1 percent of the Bible's total words.[2]

That information helps us to appreciate the worth, the import, of the twenty words this little maid from Israel speaks in this biblical account. This child, who had suffered being captured by the enemy of her people and taken away from her family into a foreign place, not only kept her faith but made an effort to speak to her mistress and tell her of a prophet who could cure her husband Naaman—the mighty commander of the army of the king of Syria, who happened to have leprosy!

Naaman repeated this little maid's words to his king. Her words then prompted the king of Syria to send Naaman on his way to Samaria with a letter to the king of Israel—another high-ranking individual who would

2 Antonia Blumberg, "This Is How Many Words Are Spoken by Women in the Bible," HuffPost, February 4, 2015, https://www.huffpost.com/entry/bible-women-words_n_6608282.

be reading the advice of a little maid from Israel forced to serve in Syria!

One might wonder why this little girl would want her captor to benefit in any way, shape, or form. Perhaps her time would have been spent more wisely figuring out how she might escape her circumstances. Instead, prompted by God's love and compassion, she acted out of affection for her mistress and shared her knowledge of how her husband might find healing from that same God.

In other words, the little maid wanted to be a blessing to those she served. For her, there was no looking back, no wallowing in misery. Instead, she moved forward in love and compassion.

No matter where you find yourself in life, no matter how many bad breaks you believe you've suffered, be like this little servant girl. Make your words count by speaking in faith from a loving heart.

....

....

....

....

....

....

....

....

....

....

....

....

Lord, may I move forward in love and compassion. May my words lead others to You.

Day 27

THE LITTLE MAID AND THE MIGHTY MAN: PART 2

[Naaman] went in and told his king, Thus and thus said the maid from Israel. And the king of Syria said, Go now, and I will send a letter to the king of Israel. And he departed and took with him ten talents of silver, 6,000 shekels of gold, and ten changes of raiment.
2 KINGS 5:4–5 AMPC

Naaman took seriously the advice of his wife's young maid from Israel. He firmly believed that the prophet in Samaria could cure him of his skin disease. Thus, he and his servants traveled to Samaria, met the king of Israel, and eventually made their way to the prophet Elisha. Naaman stood at the door of Elisha's house, but the prophet didn't personally come to speak to him. Instead, he sent a messenger to tell Naaman, "Go wash seven times in the Jordan and your flesh will be restored and you will be clean" (2 Kings 5:10 HCSB).

The fact that Naaman was not granted a face-to-face meeting with Elisha infuriated him: "I was telling myself: He will surely come out, stand and call on the name of Yahweh his God, and will wave his hand over the spot and cure the skin disease" (verse 11 HCSB). For this kind of treatment, Naaman figured he could have stayed home and taken a dip in one of the rivers there! He exclaimed in frustration, "Aren't Abana and Pharpar, the rivers of Damascus, better than all the waters of Israel? Could I not wash in them and be clean?" (verse 12 HCSB).

Fortunately, Naaman's servants talked some sense into their master, saying, "My father, if the prophet had told you to do some great thing, would you not have done it? How much more should you do it when he tells you, 'Wash and be clean'?" (verse 13 HCSB).

So Naaman acquiesced to dipping himself in the Jordan. After doing so, his skin was indeed restored! Naaman then reported back to Elisha, declaring that he knew there was "no God in the whole world except in Israel" (verse 15 HCSB). Although Elisha refused to accept the gift Naaman offered for his services, the prophet did leave Naaman with a blessing, telling him, "Go in peace" (verse 19 HCSB).

When God's answer to your prayer or His remedy for your predicament is not what you expected, don't let your pride keep you from receiving His cure for what ails you and His blessing of peace.

....

....

....

....

....

....

....

....

....

....

....

....

....

....

Lord, thank You for all the blessings, all the remedies, You bring my way.

Day 28

COMING TO JESUS

He threw off his coat, jumped up, and came to Jesus. Then Jesus answered him, "What do you want Me to do for you?"
MARK 10:50–51 HCSB

A blind beggar by the name of Bartimaeus was sitting on the roadside. From the crowd he learned that Jesus was passing by. Not knowing exactly where Jesus was, Bartimaeus began to yell, "Son of David, Jesus, have mercy on me!" (Mark 10:47 HCSB).

The people around him tried to shush him. But the blind man would not be silenced. In fact, he began yelling even louder for Jesus to have mercy on him.

The beggar's pleas stopped Jesus in His tracks. He told those around Him, "Call him" (verse 49 HCSB). They did so, telling Bartimaeus to have courage and rise up because Jesus was calling him.

The blind man threw off his coat and ran to Jesus. When Jesus asked him what he wanted Him to do, Bartimaeus answered, "I want to see!" (verse 51 HCSB). Jesus replied, "Go your way. . . . Your faith has healed you" (verse 52 HCSB).

In that moment, Bartimaeus regained his sight and began to follow Jesus down the road.

This account teaches us several things. First, Jesus' name awakens the hope within. For we know the miracles He has done in the lives of others, a list of names we would want ours included in.

Second, hearing that Jesus' presence is among us, we acknowledge that we don't want Him to pass us by. We refuse to allow those around us to deter us from petitioning Him. In our eagerness to reach Him, we cannot help but call out to Him, asking Him to see us, to love us, to meet our need, even though we may not be able to see Him.

Third, when Jesus does notice us, when He calls us to Him, we don't want to trip ourselves up. We don't want to stumble on our way to His side. So we must throw off any outer (or inner) impediment that may trip us up.

Fourth, when we reach Jesus and He asks us what we want Him to do for us, we are to recognize Jesus for who He is—our Healer, Teacher, and Master—and answer Him with our deepest need: to have our eyes opened so that we may see Him.

Lastly, when Jesus has granted our request and opened our eyes to His presence, we must continue to follow after Him, to learn what He would have us understand and know.

....

....

....

....

....

....

....

....

....

....

....

....

....

Here I am, Lord. Open my eyes that I may see You, love You, follow You.

Day 29

ALWAYS THERE

So John was beheaded in the prison. . . . Later, John's disciples came for his body and buried it. Then they went and told Jesus what had happened. As soon as Jesus heard the news, he left in a boat to a remote area to be alone. But the crowds heard where he was headed and followed on foot.
MATTHEW 14:10, 12–13 NLT

Young mothers know what it's like to try to find time alone. It can be extremely difficult when the children are very young. For little ones cannot seem to tolerate any barrier, any closed door between them and the person they count on for love, protection, feeding, and so much more.

Thus, we can just imagine what Jesus was experiencing in today's account. His cousin John the Baptist had been beheaded. His disciples buried his body then sent word to Jesus. Upon hearing the news, Jesus left by boat, wanting to be somewhere He could grieve, think things out, and, most importantly, commune with God.

That one-on-one time with the Lord is so precious. For it's there we find our strength, power, and comfort. It's there we determine our next steps. But on this occasion, as Jesus sought alone time with His Father by getting away in a boat, the crowds followed Him. . .on foot. Then, "as He stepped ashore, He saw a huge crowd, felt compassion for them, and healed their sick" (Matthew 14:14 HCSB).

The stretching of Jesus' patience and energy continued into the evening. That's when His disciples told Him to send the people away so they could find food. Jesus had another idea. He told the disciples to feed the people themselves.

The Twelve gave Jesus the meager supply they had: five loaves of bread and two fishes. He told everyone to sit down, looked up to heaven, blessed the loaves and fishes, and then gave the food to the disciples to distribute. Not only were all five thousand men, along with women and children, fed, but there were twelve baskets of leftovers!

Finally, after expending all that energy healing and feeding the people, Jesus sent them away. Once more He went off by Himself and finally found a place to pray alone.

Jesus understands your tiredness. He gets the fact that you can rarely find a moment alone, a place where you will have no interruptions. But He wants you to know that no matter what the hour, what the need, He will drop all else—even His own grief and alone time—to love you, help you, and feed you. Just as a mother would her child.

Lord, thank You for always being there for me!

Day 30

TIMING

To every thing there is a season, and a time to every purpose under the heaven: a time to be born, and a time to die; a time to plant, and a time to pluck up that which is planted; a time to kill, and a time to heal; a time to break down, and a time to build up; a time to weep, and a time to laugh; a time to mourn, and a time to dance; a time to cast away stones, and a time to gather stones together; a time to embrace, and a time to refrain from embracing.
ECCLESIASTES 3:1–5 KJV

There are certain things in this world we cannot alter, rearrange, or run ahead of. God has created this world above and below. He has put things in the order in which He wants them. He works out every happening on His own timetable. Just as we cannot force spring to come in the winter months, we cannot force joy to come to us until our mourning is over.

But even though we can't alter what God has set in place, we can find a way to endure, to remain patient. For if we don't, we'll only end up giving birth to future troubles.

Consider Abraham's wife Sarah. God had promised her and Abraham a son and a multitude of descendants. Year after year passed, and still no seed was planted within her womb. Finally, Sarah's patience ran out. She told Abraham to take her maid Hagar as a surrogate. He did.

Together Abraham and Hagar conceived a child they named Ishmael. Eventually Sarah, through Abraham, birthed Isaac. And it was these two sons whose descendants would become warring factions that are still battling things out today. For Ishmael is the father of the Arabs and an ancestor of Muhammad, while Isaac is a father of Israel and an ancestor of Moses and Jesus.

There are some things we can neither rush nor avoid. Things good and bad, easy and difficult will come into our lives as a matter of course. And our best strategy is to accept those things, knowing that God is with us as we endure them. That He will turn whatever we suffer into something good. That God truly does know best and "hath made every thing beautiful in his time" (Ecclesiastes 3:11 KJV).

Help me accept and endure all my times here on earth, Lord, knowing You walk with me through them.

Day 31

OPENED EYES

"Don't be afraid!" Elisha told him. "For there are more on our side than on theirs!" Then Elisha prayed, "O LORD, open his eyes and let him see!" The LORD opened the young man's eyes, and when he looked up, he saw that the hillside around Elisha was filled with horses and chariots of fire.
2 KINGS 6:16–17 NLT

The king of Aram (Syria) was miffed. No matter where or when he sent his troops into Israel, the king of Israel was prepared to defend his kingdom in that exact place and at that exact time. Finally, the king of Aram asked who among his officers was the traitor, the one "informing the king of Israel of my plans" (2 Kings 6:11 NLT). One of his officers told him, "Elisha, the prophet in Israel, tells the king of Israel even the words you speak in the privacy of your bedroom!" (verse 12 NLT).

Angry at the impertinence of the prophet, the king commanded his men to find out where Elisha was so that he could capture him. When it was discovered Elisha was at a city called Dothan, the king of Aram sent a huge army with many chariots and horses to Dothan. They surrounded the city at night.

The following morning, Elisha's servant went outside. He saw horses and chariots everywhere he looked. Panicked, he ran back into the house and asked Elisha, "Oh, sir, what will we do now?" (verse 15 NLT).

Elisha told his servant not to fear, for there were far more on their side than in the forces of the king of Aram. Elisha then prayed for God to open his servant's eyes. When He did so, the young man saw the hillside filled with horses and chariots of fire!

Earthly troubles tend to pull us into the flesh. But God would have us always remember to turn to Him in trouble, to go to Him with our fears, to ask Him to open our eyes so that we might see the heavenly reality of our earthly situation.

In what areas of your own life are you feeling afraid or overwhelmed? Where might you have some blind spots, not understanding that God is working in your situation?

Today, go to God. Ask Him whatever questions are burning in your mind, fueling your fears, and feeding your panic. Request that the Lord would open your eyes so that you may see things from His perspective, that you might observe where and how He is protecting you.

....

....

....

....

....

....

....

....

....

....

....

....

....

....

Dear Lord, thank You for working in my life, for opening my eyes, for protecting me, for calming my fears. Amen.

Day 32

WATER WALKERS

He went up into the hills by himself to pray. Night fell while he was there alone. Meanwhile, the disciples were in trouble far away from land, for a strong wind had risen, and they were fighting heavy waves. About three o'clock in the morning Jesus came toward them, walking on the water.
MATTHEW 14:23–25 NLT

Having again found some time alone, Jesus had to tear Himself away from the presence of His Father. For His disciples were in a boat being pummeled by the wind and waves.

Finally, they saw someone (or perhaps more like something) walking on the water toward them. The men panicked and in fear cried out, "It's a ghost!" (Matthew 14:26 NLT).

To quell their fears, Jesus immediately yelled out, "Take courage!" He identified Himself as "I AM!" then commanded them to "stop being afraid!" (verse 27 AMPC).

Their fears generally allayed at this point, Peter said, "Lord, if it is You, command me to come to You on the water" (verse 28 AMPC). Jesus did so.

So Peter climbed over the side of the boat and began walking on the water toward Jesus.

"But when he perceived and felt the strong wind, he was frightened, and as he began to sink, he cried out, Lord, save me [from death]!" (verse 30 AMPC). Immediately, Jesus reached out to Peter, caught him in His arms, and said, "O you of little faith, why did you doubt?" (verse 31 AMPC).

As the two men climbed into the boat, the storm ceased. Seeing that Jesus had the power to calm the wind and waves, the disciples then and there realized He was truly the Son of God.

This account is a reminder that as a believer and follower of Jesus, you can expect He will be there whenever you're in trouble, coming in whatever form, whatever way, and whatever time He deems best.

Because Jesus is the Great I Am, God incarnate, rest in the assurance that there is nothing He cannot or will not do to protect and save you. All you need to do is remember that truth and take courage from it.

When Jesus commands you to do something and you dare to meet that challenge, remember to keep your eyes on Him—not on all the dangers that surround you—assured by your faith that Jesus will keep you from all harm. And know that if you are in dire straits, He will respond immediately to your cries for help.

....

....

....

....

....

....

....

....

....

....

....

....

....

Lord, make me a water walker, knowing You are riding the waves with me!

Day 33

THAT ONE THING

One thing have I asked of the Lord, that will I seek, inquire for, and [insistently] require: that I may dwell in the house of the Lord [in His presence] all the days of my life, to behold and gaze upon the beauty [the sweet attractiveness and the delightful loveliness] of the Lord and to meditate, consider, and inquire in His temple.

PSALM 27:4 AMPC

When Jesus was at Martha's house, she was so busy and distracted by serving that she didn't have the time or brain space to sit near, listen to, and learn from Jesus. But her sister Mary did. When Martha later asked Jesus to tell Mary to help her, Jesus instead told Martha that Mary had chosen the better thing, the one thing necessary (Luke 10:41–42).

To escape worry about the future and the anxiety and stress it brings with it, Jesus told His followers not to worry but to seek first one thing: the kingdom of God. Then all the rest would be provided for them (Matthew 6:33).

Then, in regard to one solitary endeavor, the apostle Paul reminded his readers, "One thing I do [it is my one aspiration]: forgetting what lies behind and straining forward to what lies ahead, I press on toward the goal to win the [supreme and heavenly] prize to which God in Christ Jesus is calling us upward" (Philippians 3:13–14 AMPC).

Then here, in Psalm 27, we are once more confronted with that "one thing." The one thing its author asked of God was to seek God, to dwell with Him in His presence, to behold Him and meditate upon Him in His temple all the days of his life.

God loves people who are striving for that one thing. The woman who sits at His feet, gazing up at Him with love and joy, longing and waiting for His touch. The woman who puts Him first. The woman who above all other things desires to hear what God has to say, sinking deep into His Word, taking all she can out, treasuring and pondering those things in her heart. When you strive for that one thing, not looking back, forgetting about the past, and only living in the present with Jesus by your side, then you will realize you have no one and nothing to fear. And the calming peace of Jesus will permeate you within and without.

....

....

....

....

....

....

....

....

....

....

....

....

....

Lord, one thing I live for, one thing I seek:
You, Your continual presence and Word!
For then I'll be able to say to myself,
"When besieged, I'm calm as a baby.
When all hell breaks loose, I'm collected
and cool" [Psalm 27:3 MSG].

Day 34

THAT POSITIVE ATTITUDE

[What, what would have become of me] had I not believed that I would see the Lord's goodness in the land of the living! Wait and hope for and expect the Lord; be brave and of good courage and let your heart be stout and enduring. Yes, wait for and hope for and expect the Lord.
PSALM 27:13–14 AMPC

There have been and will be times when we're unable to stand tall and keep our footing. One moment we're caught up in the current or fighting off the undertow, and the next thing we know a big wave has taken us down. We come up coughing and sputtering, only to be hit head-on by another swell of seawater.

Yet we belong to and seek the face of a God who not only can calm the wind and waves and break us free from the undertow but can actually walk on water! And help us to do the same!

That's why, when we're feeling down, when trouble seems to be assailing us from every angle, when we're finding it difficult to catch even a little bit of a break, we can cling to the words of Psalm 27:13–14.

When we're in dire straits, we can believe in God's goodness. We can expect that we will see something good coming out of all the messes we're in, no matter the amount or type of trouble currently engulfing us. As long as we believe we will see God's goodness in this life we are living, we will find the peace we need to persevere. We will find the patience to not just survive but thrive in Him. Waiting for, hoping for, and expecting God to bring us good will give us the courage we need to continue on, day after day, night after night, step after step.

Know that God does indeed hear your voice and will answer you

(Psalm 27:7). That even if your parents abandon you (whether that means they have walked away or passed away), God will always be there for you (verse 10), caring for you better than they ever could. Know that God will show you the path you should take and lead you where He would have you go until you have found a place of safety (verses 11–12).

Today, no matter what's happening in your life, commit the words of Psalm 27:13–14 to memory. Then when trouble strikes, you'll be ready to handle it with God by your side.

....

....

....

....

....

....

....

....

....

....

....

....

....

....

....

....

I expect to see Your goodness, Lord. In You I wait and hope!

Day 35

DO GOOD

Don't worry about the wicked or envy those who do wrong. For like grass, they soon fade away. Like spring flowers, they soon wither. Trust in the LORD *and do good. Then you will live safely in the land and prosper.*
PSALM 37:1–3 NLT

King Saul hated, haunted, and hunted David. Day after day, David found himself on the run, hiding from Saul, his spies, and his soldiers in the wilderness.

On one occasion Saul, who was seeking David in the wilderness of En-gedi, went into a cave to relieve himself. Amazingly enough, David and his men were hiding in that same cave.

As Saul was relieving himself, David's men said to him, "Look, this is the day the LORD told you about: 'I will hand your enemy over to you so you can do to him whatever you desire' " (1 Samuel 24:4 HCSB). Hearing the logic of these words, David got up then stealthily cut off part of Saul's robe.

But afterward, David's conscience pricked him because of what he had done. To his men he said, "I swear before the LORD: I would never do such a thing to my lord, the LORD's anointed. I will never lift my hand against him, since he is the LORD's anointed" (verse 6 HCSB). These words stopped his men in their tracks so that no other hand or weapon was raised against Saul.

Not only that but David rose up, followed Saul out of the cave, and then bowed down, addressing Saul as "my lord the king" (verse 8 HCSB). David explained what had happened, how he'd reached out and cut off Saul's robe and been encouraged to take this opportunity to kill Saul. Yet he dared not harm the Lord's anointed. David continued, saying, "May the LORD judge between you and me, and may the LORD take vengeance on you for me, but my hand will never be against you. As the old proverb says, 'Wickedness comes from wicked people.' My hand will never be against you" (verses 12–13 HCSB).

King Saul broke into tears. He admitted to David, "You are more upright in God's eyes than I, for you have repaid me good, but I have rewarded you evil" (verse 17 AMPC). The two men then parted ways.

No matter how hounded we are by evil people and their evil desires, we must remember that God would have us not just depart from evil and do good (Psalm 37:27) but actually repay evil with good (Romans 12:17–21; 1 Peter 3:9).

Why? Because God is all about love and goodness.

....

....

....

....

....

....

....

....

....

....

....

....

....

....

Lord, help me to continue to do good and follow You.

Day 36

WAIT EXPECTANTLY

Commit your way to the Lord; trust in Him, and He will act. . . . Be silent before the Lord and wait expectantly for Him; do not be agitated by one who prospers in his way, by the man who carries out evil plans.
Psalm 37:5, 7 HCSB

Once again, David had a chance to do some real harm to his lord and king, Saul, the one relentlessly running after David, determined to kill him.

Saul headed into the wilderness of Ziph with three thousand men to seek out David. The king decided to camp on a hill. David's spies gave him Saul's exact location. That night, David and one of his men, Abishai, went to the hill of Hachilah and saw where Saul and his men lay sleeping deeply. Saul's spear was stuck in the ground by his head.

Abishai said to David, "Today God has handed your enemy over to you. Let me thrust the spear through him into the ground just once. I won't have to strike him twice!" (1 Samuel 26:8 HCSB), but once again, David (who, like Saul, had also been anointed king by Samuel) refused to lift a hand against another of the Lord's anointed. David added, "As the Lord lives, the Lord will certainly strike him down: either his day will come and he will die, or he will go into battle and perish" (verse 10 HCSB). In other words, David need not worry about killing Saul. He trusted that the Lord Himself would do so.

But there was one thing he would do and did do: he took Saul's spear and jug of water. Once he and Abishai were a safe distance from Saul and his men, David yelled down to Saul's commander Abner, telling him that he had taken Saul's spear and water. That Abner and his men should be better protectors of Saul, the Lord's anointed.

David then asked Saul why he kept pursuing him, an innocent man.

Saul admitted his missteps, saying that he was a fool, that he would never try to harm David again because David had considered Saul's life precious.

David and Saul once again parted ways. But David still avoided Saul, placing no confidence in the king's confessions or promises. He simply waited patiently for providence to play its part.

Do as David, the author of Psalm 37 and the man who would become Saul's successor as king, did. Trust that God's plan for your life is already in process. Then put all your trust in Him and wait patiently for Him to play His hand.

I patiently await You, Lord.

Day 37

ENCOURAGED IN THE LORD

David was greatly distressed, for the men spoke of stoning him because the souls of them all were bitterly grieved, each man for his sons and daughters. But David encouraged and strengthened himself in the Lord his God.
1 Samuel 30:6 AMPC

David wasn't sure how long his good fortune would hold out against the murderous Saul. So David ran where he thought the king would not follow—into the enemy territory of the Philistines. David took his six hundred men and two wives with him. And the Philistines agreed to give David the town of Ziklag in which to reside.

David's strategy paid off, at least temporarily, because when Saul heard he'd fled to Gath, he no longer chased after him. But later, when the Philistine forces were about to battle Israel, David and his men were commanded to go back home, for the Philistines no longer trusted David's loyalty.

So David and his men headed home to their families in Ziklag. When they arrived, they found that the Amalekites had raided their village, burned it with fire, and taken not just all the animals but all the people—including the men's wives and children—with them.

"David and the men with him lifted up their voices and wept until they had no more strength to weep" (1 Samuel 30:4 AMPC). Circumstances then took a dangerous turn. For the men were so full of sorrow and anger that they began talking of stoning David.

So David turned to God, not just for mental and emotional support but for guidance. He asked God what he should do, God answered him, and David followed His directions (verses 7–9). In the end, David not only recovered everything the Amalekites had taken, including all the wives and children, but also came back with his enemy's flocks and herds!

Most people in this earthly life come up against some very difficult situations, ones in which we never dreamed we'd find ourselves. At those times, we can be so overcome with grief that we begin to think not only irrationally but irreverently. Instead of leaving things in God's hands, we start contemplating how to avenge ourselves and our loved ones.

But instead of looking for revenge, we, like David, should be looking to God. For in Him we'll find not just comfort, encouragement, and strength but justice—and so much more besides!

May I turn to You, Lord, when hard days come, and from You receive the strength and encouragement I need.

Day 38

URGED AND PROMPTED BY FAITH

[Urged on] by faith Abraham, when he was called, obeyed and went forth to a place which he was destined to receive as an inheritance; and he went, although he did not know or trouble his mind about where he was to go. [Prompted] by faith he dwelt as a temporary resident in the land which was designated in the promise [of God, though he was like a stranger] in a strange country.
HEBREWS 11:8–9 AMPC

Hebrews 11:1 makes it clear that faith is the reality of what we hope for, the proof of what we do not see. And it is by this faith that we understand that God's word created everything around us and that "what we see was not made out of things which are visible" (Hebrews 11:3 AMPC).

Hebrews then provides a wonderful list of the things that faith prompted or urged the faithful to do. Looking down that list, we find Abraham. He's the man to whom God promised a specific area of land, along with descendants too numerous to count who would dwell in that land. God also promised that His plan for that land for Abraham and his descendants would ultimately become a blessing to all people!

God made those amazing promises to Abraham, a man who truly believed and was fully assured that God would do what He said He would do. No ifs, ands, or buts about it. Imagine God calling you to leave your home and all the people you know to go to a place you'd never seen or heard of before. Imagine having so much faith that you follow God's command without a second thought. Like Abraham, you sense your faith continually urging you on, through each seeming setback, keeping you forever moving forward.

Where has God worked in your life? To what places or ventures has He called you, without your actually knowing or being able to envision where you were going or what you'd be doing? How little or how much was your mind troubled by this not knowing?

When Abraham embarked upon this journey of faith, chances are he didn't imagine he'd have a trouble-free life from here on out. But perhaps what kept Abraham, the sojourner in a strange land, going was the certainty that no matter where he went, God would be walking with him. That no matter what happened, in the end he would find that God stayed true to His word.

Lord of all, I am Your obedient servant.
Give me the faith to go wherever
and whenever You call me.
Make me a faith walker.

Day 39

BECAUSE OF FAITH

Because of faith also Sarah herself received physical power to conceive a child, even when she was long past the age for it, because she considered [God] Who had given her the promise to be reliable and trustworthy and true to His word. So from one man, though he was physically as good as dead, there have sprung descendants whose number is as the stars of heaven and as countless as the innumerable sands on the seashore.
HEBREWS 11:11–12 AMPC

In this long list of people of faith, we see Sarah's name. This is the woman who had a hard time believing she and Abraham, an elderly couple, would ever have a child.

At one point, Sarah, perhaps tired of waiting for God to keep His promise, finagled things so that Abraham took her maid Hagar as a surrogate wife, thinking she'd get her child that way (Genesis 16). But Sarah's scheme didn't work out at all as she had planned.

Then the Lord came to visit Abraham and repeated His promise that he and Sarah would have a child by the same time next year. On this occasion, Sarah, whose time for conceiving and birthing babies was well past, overheard the Lord's remark and laughed, saying to herself, "After I have become shriveled up and my lord is old, will I have delight?" (Genesis 18:12 HCSB).

Sarah's laugh prompted God to ask Abraham, "Why did Sarah laugh, saying, 'Can I really have a baby when I'm old?' Is anything impossible for the LORD? At the appointed time I will come back to you, and in about a year she will have a son" (verses 13–14 HCSB).

Not only did Sarah disrespect God by laughing at the improbability that she and Abraham would have a child together, but then she lied about having laughed (verse 15)!

Nonetheless, we read in Hebrews 11:11 that because of her faith, Sarah was given the power to conceive a child. Why? Because despite her missteps, Sarah's faith in God and in His commitment to His word overcame any doubt and incredulity she may have had.

You too can be a woman of faith, one who will receive the power to be the woman God created you to be. Perhaps you too have experienced times of incredulity. But God wants you to know, to remember, to be confident in the fact that nothing is impossible for Him. Whatever He has called you to, He will make a way for His promise to become your reality. All you need to do is add your faith.

Here I am, Lord. Fill me with faith!

Day 40

ETERNAL WORDS

As the rain and snow come down from the heavens, and return not there again, but water the earth and make it bring forth and sprout, that it may give seed to the sower and bread to the eater, so shall My word be that goes forth out of My mouth: it shall not return to Me void [without producing any effect, useless], but it shall accomplish that which I please and purpose, and it shall prosper in the thing for which I sent it.
ISAIAH 55:10–11 AMPC

God promises that whatever He says will produce the intended result. That it will accomplish what He wants it to accomplish.

Jesus said the same thing! When telling His followers what the last days would be like, He reminded them that His words would never fade or pass away. He said that even when heaven and earth pass away, His words will remain.

What does that mean for us today?

All the promises God has made us, all the happenings the prophets foretold, all the prayers the apostles and scribes penned, all the psalms that have been sung, all the words that appear at your fingertips in the Holy Book of God will continue in their power and might forever and ever.

So you can stop worrying. You can take up the sword of the Spirit (that is, God's Word; Ephesians 6:17) and use it to defend yourself against and overpower the forces of evil. You can sink your soul into and assume ownership of the words Jesus prayed, not just for the believers who followed Him but for we who later would come to believe in Him (John 17:20–23).

You can take up the blessing Jesus spoke for those who believed but never saw Him, for those who "adhered to and trusted and relied on" Him, yet never met Him face-to-face, hand to hand (John 20:29 AMPC).

All the promises in the Bible—Old Testament and New—you may claim for yourself every day. You can remind yourself that God's promises never failed the Israelites (Joshua 21:45) and will never fail you; that God is always with you (Joshua 1:9); that He designed you for a specific purpose (Ephesians 2:10) and has a specific plan for you (Jeremiah 29:11); that He hears your prayers, answering them while you're still speaking (Isaiah 65:24); and that He will always guide you (Psalm 73:24) and direct your path (Proverbs 3:6).

Here's your challenge: Find a promise. Etch it on your heart and mind. Then watch it become a reality.

Lord, write Your eternal words upon my heart.

Day 41

A POWERFUL PRAYER PATTERN

People came and told Jehoshaphat, "A vast number from beyond the Dead Sea and from Edom has come to fight against you; they are already in Hazazon-tamar" (that is, En-gedi). Jehoshaphat was afraid, and he resolved to seek the Lord.
2 Chronicles 20:2–3 HCSB

Jehoshaphat was a good and humble king of Judah. Hearing that massive enemy armies were coming against him and his people, Jehoshaphat was afraid. But he knew just what to do: he "set himself [determinedly, as his vital need] to seek the Lord" (2 Chronicles 20:3 AMPC).

Jehoshaphat told all his people to fast. Then he told them to come together to ask God for help. And when they did, he prayed to God.

Jehoshaphat began by reminding God, himself, and his people of who God was—the Lord of heaven who ruled over all nations; the one whose power and might were so great that no one and nothing could conquer Him—and of all He had done.

The king then told God what was happening in his life and the lives of his people, that huge armies were coming against them. Then he admitted to God, "We have no might to stand against this great company that is coming against us. We do not know what to do, but our eyes are upon You" (verse 12 AMPC).

This humble, heartfelt prayer spoken by Jehoshaphat in the presence of God's people was so sincere and effective that the Spirit of the Lord spoke through Jahaziel, a Levite present in the assembly. God said, "Hearken, all Judah, you inhabitants of Jerusalem, and you King Jehoshaphat. The

Lord says this to you: Be not afraid or dismayed at this great multitude; for the battle is not yours, but God's" (verse 15 AMPC).

How effective might your own prayers be if you patterned them after Jehoshaphat's by following these four steps?

1. See God in your life as your vital need and determine to seek His face.
2. Remind yourself of who God is, of all the wonderful things He has done, and of the incomparable and unconquerable power He has wielded or granted His children to wield as recorded in the scriptures.
3. Tell God the details of what's happening in your life and why you're coming to Him in prayer.
4. Admit that you have no strength or knowledge of what to do but that your eyes are upon Him.

Then wait for God to speak.

....

....

....

....

....

....

....

....

....

....

....

I come seeking You, Lord, as my vital need. My eyes are upon You. Hear my prayer!

Day 42

THE COMBINED POWER OF PRAYER AND PRAISE

Tomorrow go down to them. . . . You shall not need to fight in this battle; take your positions, stand still, and see the deliverance of the Lord [Who is] with you, O Judah and Jerusalem. Fear not nor be dismayed. Tomorrow go out against them, for the Lord is with you.
2 CHRONICLES 20:16–17 AMPC

God responded in a big way to King Jehoshaphat's prayer. And on this occasion, He told His followers that they wouldn't need to fight this battle. All God required them to do was to take their positions, stand still, and watch Him deliver them from the three armies that had come against them!

God's Spirit then reminded the king and the believers in Judah not to be afraid or upset, because when they went out the next day to meet up with those who were coming against them, the Lord would be with them.

King Jehoshaphat and God's people then did what we all should do when God responds to us: they fell down, faces on the ground, and worshipped God; others rose up to praise God with a loud voice. Then they followed God's direction.

The next morning, everyone was up early. They went out as God directed. King Jehoshaphat encouraged the people, saying, "Believe in the Lord your God and you shall be established; believe and remain steadfast to His prophets and you shall prosper" (2 Chronicles 20:20 AMPC). Jehoshaphat then appointed some to sing praises to the Lord. Those singers were to go out in front of the army and praise God, thanking Him for His love and mercy.

As soon as the praises and singing began, God went to work by turning each enemy army against the other. All that remained was for Jehoshaphat and his people to take the spoil: "They found among them much cattle, goods, garments, and precious things which they took for themselves, more than they could carry away, so much they were three days in gathering the spoil" (verse 25 AMPC). On day four, the people of God gathered together and praised the Lord in what thereafter they called the Valley of Beracah (blessing).

May we all find the faith to pray to God and the courage to follow His direction to the letter. For then we will find ourselves in the valley of blessing!

You, Lord, are the one I love and praise! Be with me today as I follow and obey!

Day 43

PEACE, PATIENCE, AND PRAYER

Peter was sleeping between two soldiers, bound with two chains: and the keepers before the door kept the prison. And, behold, the angel of the Lord came upon him, and a light shined in the prison: and he smote Peter on the side, and raised him up, saying, Arise up quickly. And his chains fell off from his hands.
ACTS 12:6–7 KJV

King Herod had been attacking the church. He'd had the disciple James, the brother of John, killed by the sword. Seeing that this action pleased the Jews, Herod had Peter arrested, put in prison, and guarded. And there Peter stayed. But there was one power Herod hadn't counted on: prayer.

Although Peter was in a prison cell, bound by chains and flanked by guards on both sides, the people of his church were praying for him "without ceasing" (Acts 12:5 KJV). And those prayers prompted God to send an angel to the prison.

Light spilled into the cell. Yet neither the angel's arrival nor the light he brought with him woke Peter, who was confident God would somehow work things out. So the angel had to strike Peter on the side and say, "Quick, get up!" (verse 7 HCSB). Just then, Peter's chains fell off.

The angel told Peter to dress, put on his shoes and coat, and follow him. Peter obeyed, thinking he was dreaming.

After the angel led Peter past guard posts and the outer gate, "which opened to them by itself" (verse 10 HCSB), and then down the street a ways, he vanished into thin air. Peter then came to himself, assured that "the Lord has sent His angel and rescued me from Herod's grasp and from all that the Jewish people expected" (verse 11 HCSB).

Peter then made his way to the church at Mary's house, the place where many were praying for him. He explained to them what had happened, told them to tell the other disciples he was free, and then left.

Would that we women of the Way would have such faith that we could sleep through any calamity and rise above all chaos, confident in the knowledge that our God will extract us from or help us to endure whatever may come. Would that we would be a powerful force of prayer not only for our loved ones but for all of God's people, chained and free. Would that we would have faith that God and His angels are watching, waiting, and ready to help us.

Lord, give me the peace, patience, and prayer power I need to rise above all strain and free the chained.

Day 44

CARED FOR

Then he was afraid and arose and went for his life. . . . But he himself went a day's journey into the wilderness and came and sat down under a lone broom or juniper tree and asked that he might die. He said, It is enough; now, O Lord, take away my life.
1 KINGS 19:3–4 AMPC

Elijah the prophet had just had a mountaintop experience. He'd proven that his God alone was the one true God, for He'd answered Elijah's prayer and proved His power by sending fire to consume a water-soaked sacrifice, the altar on which it sat, and the water that filled the trench surrounding it.

Then Elijah had the prophets of Baal seized and slaughtered. After all that, Elijah predicted rain would end the three-year drought. Once it began pouring, Elijah, running on foot, raced King Ahab in his chariot for twenty miles to Jezreel.

There King Ahab's wife, Jezebel, having been told that Elijah had killed her false prophets, sent a message to him: "May the gods punish me and do so severely if I don't make your life like the life of one of them by this time tomorrow!" (1 Kings 19:2 HCSB).

Elijah knew Queen Jezebel had the power of her position behind her threat. So he found himself not only running for his life but praying God would take it!

After such a wondrous display of God's power and glory, one would assume that Elijah would have been awed by and confident in the power of his God. But one threat from the evil queen Jezebel, and the prophet, fearing for his life, ran the other direction.

We've all been there at one point or another. We've had our own mountaintop experiences but then, under the force of an evil threat or spiteful words, were brought low by fear and folded. Fortunately, on the mountaintops and in the valleys, God cares for us.

For Elijah, God allowed time for him to sleep beneath a broom tree, then sent an angel with provisions—a freshly baked loaf of bread and a jug of water. After breaking his fast, Elijah was afforded time to sleep once more. Then the angel came back again, touched him, and supplied more food and water, provisions that gave Elijah the strength to walk forty days and forty nights to the mountain of God.

Know that no matter what happens in your life, whether you're in the valley or on the mountaintop, God will take care of you.

Thank You, Lord, for loving me in the valley and on the mountaintop.

Day 45

A STILL, SMALL VOICE

The Lord was not in the wind; and after the wind an earthquake, but the Lord was not in the earthquake; and after the earthquake a fire, but the Lord was not in the fire; and after the fire [a sound of gentle stillness and] a still, small voice. When Elijah heard the voice, he wrapped his face in his mantle and went out and stood in the entrance of the cave.

1 KINGS 19:11–13 AMPC

Elijah journeyed for forty days and forty nights to Horeb, the mountain of God. Once there, he found a cave and fell asleep. Then "the word of the Lord came to him, and He said to him, What are you doing here, Elijah?" (1 Kings 19:9 AMPC).

Elijah related to God his experience as he saw it. He got everything right except the last line, which was a mixture of truth and fiction. Elijah told God that he alone was the last of the prophets and that Jezebel was now seeking him to kill him (verse 10).

God told Elijah to stand on the mountain. Just then, the Lord passed by. A powerful wind tore at the mountains, but God wasn't in the wind. Nor was He in the earthquake or the fire that followed. But God was in the soft whisper—that still, small voice that, when he heard it, pulled Elijah to the entrance of the cave he'd sought shelter in.

Once again, God asked Elijah what he was doing there. And Elijah responded with the same words he'd used before.

God answered by telling Elijah that he was to go back the way he came (verse 15). He also gave Elijah more instructions about what to do once he'd returned. And then God told him that not every knee had bowed to Baal. In fact, more than seven thousand prophets of the one true God were left!

When God has restored your strength, He will tell you what to do next. But to hear Him, you must listen, and listen well, for His still, small voice. He may tell you to return the way you came, to step back into the situation and among the people you had been running from in fear. At the same time, He'll let you know where you've gone wrong in your thinking and assumptions. He'll give you the strength, power, and words you need to continue or finish His mission for you.

Lord, open my ears, heart, and mind to Your still, small voice.

Day 46

RETURNING AND REST

For thus said the Lord God, the Holy One of Israel: In returning [to Me] and resting [in Me] you shall be saved; in quietness and in [trusting] confidence shall be your strength. But you would not, and you said, No! We will speed [our own course] on horses!
ISAIAH 30:15–16 AMPC

In Leviticus, God gave His people two choices: If they obeyed and trusted Him, He would bless them. And part of that blessing included abundance, security, peace, calm, contentment, safety, victory over their enemies, freedom, and the presence of God (Leviticus 26:3–13). If they disobeyed and distrusted Him, the exact opposite would be the result (verses 14–33).

The same holds true today.

God knows you can't handle life (and death) on your own. So He invites you to draw close to Him, to rest in Him. That means coming to Him with all your fears. Turning over to Him all your anxious cares. Trusting in Him more than other people, relying on Him more than you would the biggest bank balance or house, the fastest or most fuel-efficient car.

When you do rely on God, when you have the faith to trust in Him, turning over to Him all you have, love, and care for, then you will find your soul quieted, a heavenly stillness beyond compare. Your desires will be subdued and calmed.

And along with this trust in Him, this rest from the world's woes, and this quietness of spirit, you will find the confidence you've been longing for. You'll know that whatever happens in your life, God will be with you, watching out for you, saving you. And in that confidence, you will discover that heavenly strength that comes only when a person trusts in God.

None of this means you'll have a trouble-free life. You'll still have the upsets and griefs that accompany life on this earth. But God will be walking with you through them. Your eyes and ears, your heart and spirit will be attuned to Him.

Many people in Old Testament times trusted in wealth, fast horses, or solid chariots to keep them safe. And, like the Egyptians at the Red Sea, they were swept away. But those who confidently trusted in the Lord received His blessing.

Today, ask God to help you put all things under His care so that you too will find the rest, calm, confidence, and strength He promises.

Help me, Lord, to turn over to You my entire self, as well as all I love and possess, all I hope and dream.

Day 47

PERFECT TIMING

The Lord [earnestly] waits [expecting, looking, and longing] to be gracious to you; and therefore He lifts Himself up, that He may have mercy on you and show loving-kindness to you. For the Lord is a God of justice. Blessed (happy, fortunate, to be envied) are all those who [earnestly] wait for Him, who expect and look and long for Him [for His victory, His favor, His love, His peace, His joy, and His matchless, unbroken companionship]!

ISAIAH 30:18 AMPC

Scripture tells us that God is always waiting to bless us through His mercy, love, sense of justice, and kindness. Sometimes that waiting period can be mere hours, days, weeks, months, years. Other times it can be more than a lifetime.

We know all things happen in accordance with God's timing. What we don't know is how long we'll need to wait. Thus, what we must do is trust in God's perfect timing, for He's the one with the grand plan for each individual follower.

When the prophet Habakkuk complained to God, anxious for an answer, God told him, "The vision is yet for an appointed time and it hastens to the end [fulfillment]; it will not deceive or disappoint. Though it tarry, wait [earnestly] for it, because it will surely come; it will not be behindhand on its appointed day" (Habakkuk 2:3 AMPC).

David had a vision to build a house for God. But his hands were too bloody. So even though David was the apple of His eye, God made it clear that his son Solomon would be the one to build the house of God (1 Chronicles 28:3). And David was okay with that. After all, he trusted God with not just himself but the timing of all things. So instead of building the temple, David worked to build up whatever supplies might be needed for its construction, never living to see the house of God erect and occupied by the supernatural being he had served his entire life.

Our lives are but a breath. But how wonderful that God designs, creates, breathes life into, and uses every person to bring His plans to fruition.

How might God be using you right now? What of your life, talents, and dreams have you offered Him for His use? In what ways do you think some dreams have been put on hold? What can you do to serve Him in other ways?

Have mercy on me, Lord. Give me the patience to wait upon You for all things.

Day 48

A WORD BEHIND YOU

He will surely be gracious to you at the sound of your cry; when He hears it, He will answer you. And though the Lord gives you the bread of adversity and the water of affliction, yet your Teacher will not hide Himself any more, but your eyes will constantly behold your Teacher. And your ears will hear a word behind you, saying, This is the way; walk in it, when you turn to the right hand and when you turn to the left.
ISAIAH 30:19–21 AMPC

God hears the cries of His people. No matter where you go or where you turn, God is, has been, and always will be there for you. When open, your spiritual eyes will continually behold the Lord God. He will always be there to tell you what to do, where to go, how to live.

Consider the wise men who had seen the star rising, the star that meant the King of the Jews had been born. While on its trail, they stopped in their travels to speak with King Herod, seeing what information he might've had so they could reach the one they wanted to worship.

The wise men's visit troubled Herod. After consulting with his own contingent of sage advisors, Herod told the wise men to go to Bethlehem, for prophecy said that was where the King of the Jews was to be born. Then Herod told them to bring him word when they did find Him so that he too could go and worship Him (Matthew 2:8), meaning, "so I can come and kill Him."

So the wise men followed the rising star, found Jesus, and worshipped Him, offering Him treasures. Afterward they were "warned in a dream not to go back to Herod" (verse 12 HCSB), and so they returned to their own country by a different route.

After the wise men left, an angel of the Lord came to Joseph in a dream and told him to take Mary and Jesus and flee to Egypt. They left in the night to escape those who wanted to destroy the child. After Herod died, another angel of the Lord told Joseph to return to Israel with the mother and her child; then, hearing that Archelaus was reigning in place of his father Herod, Joseph was redirected to Nazareth.

Know that God will always be with you. And as with so many before you, He will tell you which way to go, which direction to take. Your job is to keep your eyes and ears open and submit to His instructions.

I am a woman with eyes and ears open to Your direction, Lord. Please lead me.

Day 49

EARS TO HEAR

He that hath ears to hear, let him hear. . . .
"Are you listening to me? Really listening?"
MATTHEW 11:15 KJV, MSG

It's easy to tune things out, especially sounds that are familiar. Like your pastor's voice. Or your husband's, or your kids', or your coworkers'.

That's why Jesus made a point of asking His people, "Are you really listening to Me? Do you hear what I'm saying? Are your ears even open?"

Jesus' words sound a lot like those a woman would say to her husband and children, because our family members tend to have a way of tuning us out, of exhibiting selective hearing. They seem to hear only what they want to hear, things such as "Dinnertime!" Or "Here's your allowance!" Or "I got you those cookies you like at the store today."

Meanwhile, they're completely deaf when we say things such as "Can you please take out the trash?" Or "Would you please keep the toilet seat down?" Or "Let's go! Time for church!"

You know how infuriating and frustrating it can be when your voice is ignored. Now imagine how God must feel when you turn a deaf ear to His message.

No matter where you are or what you're doing, God would have your ears open to His voice, His Word. He wants you to truly listen to what He's saying. He wants your mind open to the insights He may be trying to impart, the direction He may want to be turning you, the concept He wants you to grasp.

Someone once said, "God gave us two ears and one mouth, so we ought to listen twice as much as we speak." Do you listen to God more than you pray?

If not, God only knows how much of His message you're missing out on!

Being deaf to God's instructions is like taking a road trip with your GPS on mute. Unless you know the route, chances are good you'll find yourself lost, out in the middle of nowhere, with buzzards circling overhead.

If the Bible translation or study you're using now is not keeping your interest, consider purchasing another one. Plenty are out there. Also, make a point of going to the Lord in prayer before you listen to your pastor's message or open God's Word.

Lord, open my eyes to what You would have me see, open my ears to what You would have me hear, open my mind to what You would have me think, and open my heart to what You would have me accept.

Day 50

QUITE WILLING AND GLAD

Jesus said to them, It is I; be not afraid! [I Am; stop being frightened!] Then they were quite willing and glad for Him to come into the boat. And now the boat went at once to the land they had steered toward. [And immediately they reached the shore toward which they had been slowly making their way.]

John 6:20–21 AMPC

Imagine being one of Jesus' followers, getting into a boat, and heading out to sea. . .at night. . .in the dark. . .when Jesus isn't with you.

Next thing you know, the waves, driven by a violent wind, are getting rough and rising. No matter how much you strain at the oars, you feel as if you're fighting a losing battle. Not only are you soaked to the skin, but there's water in your shoes. You're not even sure you'll be able to hang on to the oars!

Then, just when you think things can't get any worse, some otherworldly being is heading your way! It's walking on water! Now you're not only tired, anxious, and drenched but terrified! Especially because it's heading right for you and your friends!

That's when you hear His voice. The voice of your Lord and Savior, the font of all wisdom, the source of strength, the worker of miracles. His voice is saying, "It is I; be not afraid! [I Am; stop being frightened!]"

Oh thank God! Jesus is here, you think (if not say) to yourself. Knowing it's Him, you're more than happy to invite Him into your vessel. And now, amazingly enough, you find yourself at the place to which you'd been trying to make your way! What miracle is this?

When you're in trouble, when you're at your wits' end and all your "wisdom has come to nothing" (Psalm 107:27 AMPC), cry out to God. When He answers your call, willingly allow Him into your life. He'll not only bring you out of your distresses but hush "the storm to a calm and to a gentle whisper, so that the waves of the sea are still" (verse 29 AMPC). Then you'll breathe a sigh of relief as He brings you to your "desired haven" (verse 30 AMPC), to that place you had been striving to reach but could not have reached without Him.

Here I am, Lord, adrift at sea.
Please step into my vessel.
Bring me the calm I crave. Get me
to where You would have me go!

Day 51

TIME SEEKERS

"I know the plans I have for you"—this is the Lord*'s declaration—"plans for your welfare, not for disaster, to give you a future and a hope. You will call to Me and come and pray to Me, and I will listen to you. You will seek Me and find Me when you search for Me with all your heart."*
Jeremiah 29:11–13 HCSB

Some days it can feel as if your life is not going according to your plan—or any plan, from the looks and feel of it. But God would have you know with certainty that He does have a plan for you—a good plan. One that includes hope and peace.

That's God's part.

Your part is to stay close to Him. To call to Him when things are going well and not so well. God would have you pray to Him, settling in for some "me and Thee" time—moments when He listens attentively to you, and you in return listen attentively to Him. But this special time together can't happen if you're squeezing it into your schedule. This time with God is to be quality time, time you must willingly and gladly seek with your entire heart.

You may be thinking, *But I'm a young mom. How am I ever going to find time to spend with God during my day? There's barely a minute to spare between feedings and diapers, homework and housework, and then there's my career and my calling, my love life and my work life, my church and my community.*

Busy as we are, we women, designed to nurture, seem to forget one thing: that when we do finally settle in with God, it's we who are at once nourished by the Master Nurturer! Our quiet time with God is a time during which we can receive all the love, compassion, mercy, and guidance He so abundantly gives. We then, in turn, can draw from our overflowing well of such treasures to nurture others in our lives.

Remember, Jesus said, "A thief comes only to steal and to kill and to destroy. I have come so that they may have life and have it in abundance" (John 10:10 HCSB).

So find some time in your day to seek the God who loves you and has plans for you, knowing you will get so much more back from Him than what you give to Him.

Here I am, Lord, seeking Your face, searching for You with my entire heart.

Day 52

LETTING GO

[Jochebed] a daughter of Levi. . .became pregnant and bore a son; and when she saw that he was [exceedingly] beautiful, she hid him three months. And when she could no longer hide him, she took for him an ark or basket made of bulrushes or papyrus [making it watertight by] daubing it with bitumen and pitch. Then she put the child in it and laid it among the rushes by the brink of the river [Nile].
EXODUS 2:1–3 AMPC

Having forgotten all about the amazing way that Joseph, a child of Israel, had kept the Egyptian people fed during a great famine, the new pharaoh made slaves of God's children. He did so out of fear of the great strength the Israelites had gained under God's care. He imagined that if his country went to war, the Israelites would join the Egyptians' enemies. Thus, instead of joining the Israelites in their worship of the one true God, he chose to subjugate them.

Pharaoh's fear of the Hebrews was so extreme that he told their midwives, Shiprah and Puah, to kill every male child who was born but to let the females live. Unfortunately for him, the midwives respected God more than Pharaoh, so they refused to follow his orders. When Pharaoh asked why they were not complying with his command, Shiprah and Puah said, "Hebrew women are not like the Egyptian women; they are vigorous and quickly delivered; their babies are born before the midwife comes to them" (Exodus 1:19 AMPC). Because of their words and actions, God granted them families of their own.

Meanwhile, Pharaoh, getting no help from the midwives, ordered his people to cast every Hebrew baby boy into the Nile while allowing the girls to live.

During these days, Jochebed—a daughter of one Levite, the wife of another—birthed a boy and hid him for three months. When she could hide him no longer, she carefully and lovingly built an ark, a watertight basket in which she placed then launched her beautiful baby boy—her most treasured possession who could neither feed, clothe, nor defend himself—into the crocodile-infested Nile River.

Such was the faith of this woman named Jochebed. She so trusted God that she set her precious child in His hands, on His waters, and let him go.

Have you entrusted to God that which is most precious to you?

Lord, give me the faith to put all the great treasures You have placed in my care back into Your hands.

Day 53

WAIT AND SEE

His sister [Miriam] stood some distance away to learn what would be done to him. Now the daughter of Pharaoh came down to bathe at the river, and her maidens walked along the bank; she saw the ark among the rushes and sent her maid to fetch it.
EXODUS 2:4–5 AMPC

Imagine being the big sister (anywhere between seven and fifteen years of age) to the three-month-old baby boy your mother placed in the reeds of the crocodile-infested Nile.

Miriam's faith-filled parents had trusted God to help them keep the baby hidden for three months. Now, hinging their child's welfare on God's promise to preserve His people, they set the child adrift in God's earthly arms.

Miriam's mother was wise enough to place the little ark containing her baby boy near where she knew Pharaoh's daughter bathed. And Miriam was wise enough to stand far enough away from where the baby floated so that she wouldn't be seen. Only when she saw that Pharaoh's daughter was captivated by the baby did Miriam approach the princess and her handmaids.

Miriam asked the princess, "Shall I go and call a nurse of the Hebrew women to nurse the child for you?" (Exodus 2:7 AMPC). Pharaoh's daughter quickly agreed that would be a good idea. And when Miriam brought and introduced her own mother, Jochebed, as the woman to nurse the child, Pharaoh's daughter said, "Take this child away and nurse it for me, and I will give you your wages" (verse 9 AMPC).

And that's just what Jochebed did! Once the baby had been not only weaned by his mother but taught about his heritage and faith by his

Levitical parents, Jochebed brought him back to Pharaoh's daughter. There the child whom the princess had adopted and named Moses was educated and lived in luxury.

What patience, courage, loyalty, faith, and confidence Miriam displayed at such an early age. How hard her heart must have been beating while she waited for her brother to be discovered. . .then when she approached the princess and asked if she wanted her to find a wet nurse for the child and presented her mother to the princess. How awesome to be a part of the process of patiently relying on God and reaping the blessing of that wait-and-see attitude.

May all God's daughters, big and little, young and old, develop such patience and trust.

Help me, Lord, to be wise and patient, putting all my confidence in and gaining all my courage from You.

Day 54

GOD IN THE BACKGROUND

When she opened it, she saw the child; and behold, the baby cried. And she took pity on him and said, This is one of the Hebrews' children! Then his sister said to Pharaoh's daughter, Shall I go and call a nurse of the Hebrew women to nurse the child for you?
EXODUS 2:6–7 AMPC

Never doubt what God can do through the unlikeliest of people.

Pharaoh, the king of Egypt, had commanded his people to kill all Hebrew newborn boys but to allow the newborn girls to live. Such is the scenario into which Jochebed, the daughter of one Levite and the wife of another, birthed a beautiful baby boy. After successfully keeping him hidden for three months, Jochebed then built the boy a watertight ark, placed him in it, and set it in the Nile River, near where Pharaoh's daughter usually came to bathe.

The baby's big sister, Miriam, waited out of sight to see what would happen to her brother.

When the princess came down to the river to bathe, she saw the ark and sent her maid to retrieve the basket. When the princess opened it, she saw the beautiful baby boy, who began to wail. Her heart was stolen. Even though she recognized him as "one of the Hebrews' children," it was adoration at first sight.

The next thing she knew, a little Hebrew girl was at her side, asking, "Shall I go and call a nurse of the Hebrew women to nurse the child for you?"

The princess thought that was a wonderful idea. And when the girl returned with a Hebrew woman, the child was returned to the arms of his birth mother, who was instructed to take him away and nurse him, and she would be paid for it!

Once Jochebed weaned the child, she brought him to his adoptive mother, who named him "Moses. . .because I drew him out of the water" (Exodus 2:10 AMPC). There in the palace Moses lived and was schooled by his people's enemy, the Egyptians. Later he would become a leader of God's people, a major thorn in another pharaoh's side, and the man who helped to set God's people free.

The moment the princess saw baby Moses, her compassion for another helpless human being overrode whatever edict her father had proclaimed. Love and compassion triumphed over evil, proving God can use anyone, friend or foe, to bring His plans to fruition.

Help me to remember, Lord, that You can and will use anyone to work Your will and that nothing can overpower love and compassion!

Day 55

COMPASSION-FUELED COURAGE

When Athaliah the mother of [King] Ahaziah [of Judah] saw that her son was dead, she arose and destroyed all the royal descendants. But Jehosheba, the daughter of King Jehoram, [half] sister of Ahaziah, stole Joash son of Ahaziah from among the king's sons, who were to be slain, even him and his nurse, and hid them from Athaliah.
2 Kings 11:1–2 AMPC

When a king of Egypt instructed his people to kill all male Hebrew newborns, one Levite mother, Jochebed, hid her son Moses, who eventually led his people out of Egypt and another pharaoh to his death.

Just before King Herod, hoping to kill the one born who was "king of the Jews," ordered that all male children who were two years old and under be massacred, the Lord told Joseph to take Jesus and Mary to Egypt until God told him otherwise (Matthew 2:13–16).

In between those two events, the life of another male child was in jeopardy from a cruel ruler. This time, the murderer was a woman named Athaliah. She was a queen mother, her son being King Ahaziah of Judah. When he died, Athaliah wanted the throne for herself, so she had all the royal descendants massacred. At least she *thought* she did.

As it turned out, Jehosheba, half sister of the dead king, stole one of her nephews, a baby named Joash, from the sons to be slain and hid him and his nurse for six years while Athaliah ruled as queen!

This courageous and heroic Jehosheba was wife to the priest Jehoiada (2 Chronicles 22:10–12), which is how she kept the child Joash and his nurse hidden in the house of the Lord until he was seven.

Joash's nurse showed courage as well, secluded with the royal son, protecting him until he himself, the true heir, was put on the throne. This nurse was very different from the male guardians of the sons of Ahab. For they, in fear, had the heads of all seventy of their royal charges delivered in baskets to Jehu (2 Kings 10:1–8).

Both Jehosheba and Joash's nameless nurse allowed their compassion for a child to fuel their courage to not only escape with the babe but hide him for six years from a malicious matriarch who later was slain and trampled upon by horses.

Follow the model of the good and godly Jehosheba and Joash's nurse by allowing compassion to not only fuel but sustain your courage, no matter your position or name.

Dear Lord, may my compassion override any fears I may have when I am led by Your will and endeavor to walk in Your way.

Day 56

TURN IN FAITH

But Mary remained standing outside the tomb sobbing. As she wept, she stooped down [and looked] into the tomb. And she saw two angels in white sitting there, one at the head and one at the feet, where the body of Jesus had lain. And they said to her, Woman, why are you sobbing? She told them, Because they have taken away my Lord, and I do not know where they have laid Him.

JOHN 20:11–13 AMPC

Before the sun had risen, Mary Magdalene walked to Jesus' garden tomb. The first thing she noticed was that the stone that had covered the entrance to the grave had been rolled away, and the tomb itself, like her, was bereft of Jesus.

Mary ran to Simon Peter and John, telling them, "They have taken the Lord out of the tomb, and we don't know where they have put Him!" (John 20:2 HCSB).

The two men ran to the tomb. Both witnessed it empty of Jesus, with only the dressings in which He'd been buried left behind. They then believed Mary's report but didn't understand the scriptures, nor Jesus' own announcement that He would rise from the dead. So they went home.

"But Mary remained." She wept as she stood outside the tomb then stooped to look into it. Mary saw two angels within. They asked her why she was crying.

Mary said it was because some people had taken away her Lord and she didn't know where they'd taken Him. Just then, she turned and saw Jesus standing there. He too asked her why she was crying, who she was looking for.

Mary, thinking He was the gardener, said, "Sir, if you've removed Him, tell me where you've put Him, and I will take Him away" (verse 15 HCSB).

Then Jesus simply said her name. "Mary." She turned around once more and finally recognized Him, saying, "Teacher!" (verse 16).

How many times are we so blinded by our fears, anxieties, sorrows, and tears that we don't recognize angels or the message they are trying to impart to us? On how many occasions do we not recognize Jesus, nor the fact that He is standing right beside us?

Today, open yourself to the Word. Remain there, allowing the words that touch your heart to stay with you throughout the day. Know that all you need to do is turn in faith, and you'll find the Lord you seek standing right next to you.

....

....

....

....

....

....

....

....

....

....

....

....

....

Remaining in Your Word, I turn to You, my Lord of love.

OPENED MINDS

*In the beginning [before all time] was the Word (Christ),
and the Word was with God, and the Word was God Himself. . . .
Beginning with Moses and [throughout] all the Prophets,
He went on explaining and interpreting to them in all the Scriptures
the things concerning and referring to Himself. . . . Then He
[thoroughly] opened up their minds to understand the Scriptures.*
JOHN 1:1; LUKE 24:27, 45 AMPC

Two of Jesus' disciples were heading to Emmaus, about seven miles from Jerusalem. As they walked, they discussed what had happened over the last three days. In the midst of their conversation, Jesus Himself caught up with them and began walking with them. But they didn't realize their new fellow traveler was their Lord.

When Jesus asked them what they were talking about, they told Him about the prophet Jesus of Nazareth who had performed many miracles and spoken about God to the people. How He'd been sentenced and then, just three days ago, crucified.

The men related how that very morning some female followers had told them some astounding things, unbelievable things—that Jesus' body was gone and that they'd seen angels who'd told them He was alive. But women never made good witnesses. So some of the male disciples had gone to the tomb and found things just as the women had reported.

Jesus then explained to these men, whom He described as fools, that all they had told Him had needed to happen. Then He began explaining all the things from the scriptures that connected Him to the Messiah. Later, as He broke bread with the men, their eyes were opened and they recognized Jesus. In that instant, He disappeared from their sight. That's when they said to each other, "Were not our hearts greatly moved and burning within us while He was talking with us on the road and as He opened and explained to us [the sense of] the Scriptures?" (Luke 24:32 AMPC).

The two men immediately headed back to Jerusalem to tell the other believers. While they were relating all that had happened, "Jesus Himself took His stand among them and said to them, Peace (freedom from all the distresses that are experienced as the result of sin) be to you!" (verse 36 AMPC). Later He opened up the minds of all the gathered believers so that they too could understand the scriptures.

When you need to understand the words of God, go to the Word, the source Himself. He will open your mind to what He would have you know.

....

....

....

....

....

....

....

....

....

....

....

....

Here I am, Lord. Open my mind to Your words and wisdom.

Day 58

A JOURNEY OF FAITH

"The Lord, the God of heaven, who took me from my father's house and from my native land, who spoke to me and swore to me, 'I will give this land to your offspring'—He will send His angel before you, and you can take a wife for my son from there."
GENESIS 24:7 HCSB

When Abraham was very old, he told his oldest and most loyal servant, Eliezer, to find a wife for his son Isaac. The wife was not to be one from among the Canaanites but rather from the God-fearing family of Abraham.

The servant, having packed up some of Abraham's treasures and camels, traveled to the city of Nahor. Once there, Eliezer and his camels stopped at a well. The servant then prayed:

> *"God of my master Abraham. . .give me success today, and show kindness to my master Abraham. I am standing here at the spring where the daughters of the men of the town are coming out to draw water. Let the girl to whom I say, 'Please lower your water jug so that I may drink,' and who responds, 'Drink, and I'll water your camels also'—let her be the one You have appointed for Your servant Isaac." (Genesis 24:12–14 HCSB)*

Before Eliezer had finished speaking, Rebekah, the granddaughter of Abraham's brother Nahor, arrived at the well and filled her jug. After the servant asked her for water, Rebekah not only complied with that request but offered to draw water for his camels as well.

As she performed these actions, the man simply waited silently and watched carefully "to see whether or not the LORD had made his journey a success" (verse 21 HCSB). Then he asked her who she was. When Eliezer realized she was a relative of Abraham's, he bowed down and worshipped the Lord! God had indeed sent His angel before Eliezer!

You too are a servant who has embarked on a journey. Each day God sends His angels before you, to guard you in all your ways (Psalm 91:11). He has His eyes upon you and hears the prayers you send up to Him (1 Peter 3:12). Even before you finish praying, while you're still speaking, God is acting on your behalf (Isaiah 65:24)!

Today, keep all these facts of faith at the forefront of your mind as you walk with God. Pray for His protection and blessing, and He will give you success as your will aligns with His.

"Praise the LORD. . .[who] has shown unfailing love and faithfulness" [Genesis 24:27 NLT]!

Day 59

PERPLEXITY, PRAYER, AND PROMISES

Isaac pleaded with the LORD on behalf of his wife, because she was unable to have children. The LORD answered Isaac's prayer, and Rebekah became pregnant with twins. But the two children struggled with each other in her womb. So she went to ask the LORD about it. "Why is this happening to me?" she asked.
GENESIS 25:21–22 NLT

God had promised Abraham many descendants through his and Sarah's son Isaac (Genesis 17). After Abraham had died, God vowed directly to Isaac that he would have numerous descendants (Genesis 26:4). Yet here we're told that Rebekah, Isaac's one and only wife, was barren for many years, just as Abraham's wife Sarah had been.

The aging Isaac could have just said to himself, *Well, I guess God's not going to come through for us. Might as well stop praying for an impossibility.* But he didn't. Why? Because Isaac was a man of great faith and patience. (Remember, he was the child who submissively allowed his dad to put him on an altar.) Isaac trusted God. He considered His promise a sure thing, a future fact. So Isaac continually and persistently pleaded with God to open his wife's womb. And eventually the Lord answered his prayer in a big way! Rebekah became pregnant with not one but two children! A double blessing!

Yet once Rebekah was pregnant, she noticed her babes were struggling with each other, battling it out within her womb, causing her pain. So she went to talk to God about it, asking, "Why is this happening to me?"

Here we have the first recorded instance in the Bible of a woman praying to God! Here is a woman who is suffering in her pregnancy. But instead of silently enduring not just the pain caused by the children within her but the confusion of why this was happening, she goes directly to the Master Planner, the source of our breath, love, and light.

And God answered her prayer. He told her that two children within her would become two different nations that would be rivals. One son would be stronger and the older would serve the younger, all of which would prove true.

When you have problems or feel perplexed about anything, go to God in prayer. Trust Him with all, fully assured that His promises to you are certain and true.

When I begin wondering why something is happening to me, Lord, may You be the first person I run to as I look for answers!

Day 60

POURING OUT

"I am very discouraged, and I was pouring out my heart to the LORD. Don't think I am a wicked woman! For I have been praying out of great anguish and sorrow." "In that case," Eli said, "go in peace! May the God of Israel grant the request you have asked of him."
1 SAMUEL 1:15–17 NLT

Hannah was a sweet soul, humble, tolerant, and forgiving. Perhaps the fact that she had no children grew her into that soul. For her childlessness was the defect about which her husband Elkanah's other wife (the ever-fertile Peninnah) would taunt Hannah.

Each year Elkanah would pack up the wives and kids and travel down to Shiloh. There he would worship and make a sacrifice to God before the priest Eli. Elkanah would then divvy up his portion of the offering between Peninnah and her sons and daughters. But he would give twice as much to Hannah because he loved her more, even though she was childless.

The love that Elkanah showed to Hannah irked Peninnah. So on these yearly outings to and from the tabernacle, Peninnah would tease Hannah about her barrenness to the point where Hannah could neither eat nor sleep but would simply dissolve into tears.

No one but Hannah understood her pain, the anguish she suffered. Not even her husband, who told her, "Why aren't you eating? Why be downhearted just because you have no children? You have me—isn't that better than having ten sons?" (1 Samuel 1:8 NLT).

Yet Hannah knew only one would understand what she was going through. So on one particular trip to Shiloh, Hannah got up from her uneaten plate of food and walked to the tabernacle.

Hannah knelt down and, in her distress, began to pour out her heart to the Lord. She decided to make God an offer she felt He couldn't refuse: "O Lord of Heaven's Armies, if you will look upon my sorrow and answer my prayer and give me a son, then I will give him back to you. He will be yours for his entire lifetime" (verse 11 NLT).

As Hannah prayed, all Eli the priest could see were her lips moving. Thinking she was drunk, he reprimanded her. But once Hannah helped him to understand the facts of the matter, Eli told her to go in peace, assuring her that God would answer her prayer.

When all seems against you, pour out your heart to God in prayer. He will meet you where you are.

I come before You, Lord, pouring out my heart. Please hear my prayer.

Day 61

AN ATTENTIVE LORD

The Lord paid attention to Hannah's need, and she conceived and gave birth to three sons and two daughters. Meanwhile, the boy Samuel grew up in the presence of the Lord.
1 Samuel 2:21 HCSB

After baring her soul before the Lord, Hannah took solace in Eli the priest's blessing, "May the God of Israel grant your request." With a relieved mind and a happy heart, Hannah went back to sit with her family. For the first time in ages, she could swallow her food at the sacrificial table with her husband, his other wife, and their children.

The next morning, after worship, Elkanah and his brood headed home to Ramah. "When Elkanah slept with Hannah, the Lord remembered her plea, and in due time she gave birth to a son. She named him Samuel, for she said, 'I asked the Lord for him' " (1 Samuel 1:19–20 NLT).

Over the next few years, Hannah did not take the family trip to Shiloh. She stayed home with Samuel, knowing her time with him would be limited. She told Elkanah she wanted to wait until the child was weaned before she took him to the tabernacle and dedicated him to God.

Hannah did indeed keep her promise. For when Samuel had been weaned, she, along with Elkanah and the rest of the family, took him with them down to Shiloh. After making the annual sacrifice, Hannah spoke to Eli, reminding him that she was the woman he'd seen praying to the Lord several years ago. To him she handed Samuel, the answer to her prayer, saying, "I asked the Lord to give me this boy, and he has granted my request. Now I am giving him to the Lord, and he will belong to the Lord his whole life" (verses 27–28 NLT).

The family then worshipped the Lord. And Hannah sang her song of praise and gratitude to God (1 Samuel 2:1–10), one that became the pattern for the song that Mary, the mother of Jesus, would sing thousands of years later (Luke 1:46–55).

In the years that followed, the Lord remained attentive to Hannah's needs and blessed her with more children. Meanwhile, Samuel continued to serve God and "grew in favor with the LORD and with the people" (1 Samuel 2:26 NLT).

Hannah's story reminds us that when our will is aligned with the Lord's, He will not fail. In fact, in time He will grant our greatest desires above and beyond what we hope or imagine.

Here, Lord, is my deepest desire. . . . Be attentive to my need.

Day 62

TEARS IN GOD'S BOTTLE

While Jesus was here on earth, he offered prayers and pleadings, with a loud cry and tears, to the one who could rescue him from death. And God heard his prayers because of his deep reverence for God. Even though Jesus was God's Son, he learned obedience from the things he suffered. In this way, God qualified him as a perfect High Priest, and he became the source of eternal salvation for all those who obey him.
HEBREWS 5:7–9 NLT

Shedding tears is not unseemly, unmanly, or unwomanly. Weeping doesn't mean you are weak, self-absorbed, or a crybaby. After all, Jesus Himself wept. He did so when He saw how sad people were at the death of Lazarus (John 11:35). Jesus later wept over the city of Jerusalem, which He knew would one day be destroyed because the people there "didn't recognize and welcome God's personal visit" (Luke 19:44 MSG).

Because weeping is a way of releasing your emotions of sorrow, regretfulness, and joy, your occasional shedding of tears should not be something you're ashamed of. Washington Irving wrote, "There is a sacredness in tears. They are not a mark of weakness, but of power. They speak more eloquently than ten thousand tongues. They are the messengers of overwhelming grief, of deep contrition and of unspeakable love."

According to the author of Ecclesiastes, there is a time to laugh and a time to cry (3:4). Tears and laughter are a part of life.

Abraham cried at the death of Sarah (Genesis 23:2). Hannah cried while pouring out her heart to God (1 Samuel 1:10). One woman used her tears to wet and her hair to wipe Jesus' feet (Luke 7:38).

The thing to remember is that the three-in-one God loves you like no other. He is filled with compassion for you. When you hurt, He hurts. When you cry, He is a witness to and partner in your sorrow. To Him, your tears are precious. David once wrote about God, "You keep track of all my sorrows. You have collected all my tears in your bottle. You have recorded each one in your book" (Psalm 56:8 NLT).

Yet there will come a day when God will wipe every tear from the eyes of His people. "And there will be no more death or sorrow or crying or pain. All these things are gone forever" (Revelation 21:4 NLT). Until then, if you need to cry, don't hold it in. God will see and respond with His love.

....

....

....

....

....

....

....

....

....

....

....

....

....

....

Thank You, Lord, for being the shoulder I can cry on.

Day 63

WORD POWER

Wise words are like deep waters; wisdom flows from the wise like a bubbling brook. . . . Fools' words get them into constant quarrels. . . . Wise words satisfy like a good meal; the right words bring satisfaction. The tongue can bring death or life; those who love to talk will reap the consequences.
PROVERBS 18:4, 6, 20–21 NLT

Every word you think and speak has power. What you think has power over how you live and how you view your world. The words you speak have power over other people, bringing either life or death to them. The apostle James writes that from our tongues come blessings and curses (James 3:10).

So what's a girl to do? What can we—as working women, wives, mothers, Sunday school teachers, preachers, and so forth—do to rein in our tongues so that people who hear our words are lifted up, not brought down, so that our words bring life, not death? We can tap into the wisdom of God.

Consider the wise woman of Abel. Joab, the commander of King David's army, was looking for a man named Sheba who'd supported Absalom when he was trying to wrest the throne from his father. Joab had tracked the renegade down to the city of Abel. As Joab's men began battering away at the city wall, a woman called out, asking for the men to bring Joab to her so she could speak with him.

The woman then told Joab that she was a woman of peace and of God. She asked why he was "trying to destroy a city that is like a mother in Israel" (2 Samuel 20:19 HCSB).

Joab explained that he didn't come to destroy her city but was looking for a man named Sheba who'd rebelled against their king. He then said,

"Deliver this one man, and I will withdraw from the city" (verse 21 HCSB).

The woman replied, "All right. His head will be thrown over the wall to you" (verse 21 HCSB). After the woman spoke to all the people in her city and gave them her recommendation, Sheba's head was thrown over the city wall. And Joab and his men went home.

Your words have power. So before you speak, consider what you're about to say. Ask God for His wisdom so your words will help keep the peace and save lives.

"Take control of what I say, O LORD, and guard my lips" [Psalm 141:3 NLT]. Help my words bring peace and life rather than death and strife.

Day 64

SPYING OUT THE LAND: PART 1

I told you, "You've reached the Amorite highlands, and the Eternal our God is going to give them to us soon. Look! The Eternal, your True God, has put this land within your grasp! Go up into these highlands, and take possession of them as the Eternal, the God of your ancestors, promised you would. Go! Don't be afraid, and don't be intimidated!" But you approached me with ideas of your own: "Couldn't we send a few people in to investigate first? They could explore the land, come back, and tell us what route we should take and what cities we'd come to along the way."
DEUTERONOMY 1:20–22 VOICE

From the very beginning, God's people weren't eager to head into the unknown territory comprising the Promised Land.

So Moses agreed to send twelve men, one from each tribe of Israel, to spy out the land. When they returned, loaded down with wonderful fruit from the land, the scouts said, "The land the LORD our God is giving us is good" (Deuteronomy 1:25 HCSB). But the people murmured in their tents. They not only doubted God's love for them but doubted He could give them the strength to defeat the giants who lived in that land.

The Israelites didn't even have any faith in Moses' assurance that "the LORD your God is going ahead of you. He will fight for you, just as you saw him do in Egypt. And you saw how the LORD your God cared for you all along the way as you traveled through the wilderness, just as a father cares for his child. Now he has brought you to this place" (verses 30–31 NLT).

Perhaps you've seen a wonderful opportunity before you and felt excited about embarking on it. But then you spied out the new land and decided that where you were, your current comfort zone, was the better, easier place to be. Perhaps you saw only the difficulties you might face and were blind to the grace of God that would help you through them. With seemingly insurmountable obstacles before you, you then fell back and refused to move forward, justifying your actions by reminding yourself (and perhaps others around you) that the timing just wasn't right.

Today, remember who carries you and cares for you. And move forward.

Lord, give me the faith and courage to move forward with You.

Day 65

SPYING OUT THE LAND: PART 2

They brought the Israelites an evil report of the land which they had scouted out, saying, The land through which we went to spy it out is a land that devours its inhabitants. And all the people that we saw in it are men of great stature. There we saw the Nephilim [or giants], the sons of Anak, who come from the giants; and we were in our own sight as grasshoppers, and so we were in their sight.

NUMBERS 13:32–33 AMPC

Ten of the twelve spies Moses had sent into the Promised Land came back with a grim report detailing how giants lived in that land. How they, the spies, had seen themselves as grasshoppers, and that's probably what they looked like in the eyes of those "men of great stature."

The remaining two spies, Caleb and Joshua, believed the Israelites would be more than able to conquer the Promised Land, saying:

> *If the Lord delights in us, then He will bring us into this land and give it to us, a land flowing with milk and honey. Only do not rebel against the Lord, neither fear the people of the land, for they are bread for us. Their defense and the shadow [of protection] is removed from over them, but the Lord is with us. Fear them not.* (Numbers 14:8–9 AMPC)

In the end, the Israelites sided with the ten pessimistic spies instead of Caleb and Joshua. Because God's people refused to enter the Promised Land, they became wilderness wanderers instead of faithful followers of God.

When we see God through our circumstances rather than our

circumstances through God, we too become wilderness wanderers. We, like the ten spies, compare the giants to ourselves rather than to the God of all gods.

You are a strong woman of God. You have faith in a supernatural being who claims you as His own; who has vowed to cherish, love, and safeguard you; who carries you through hardships and heartbreaks.

Your God goes before you, sends His angels to protect you, and promises you life everlasting. Your only part is to love Him and obey Him above everyone and everything else and in all circumstances.

Today, consider how you see yourself in this world and how you see God compared to the challenges and obstacles before you. Then make whatever adjustments are necessary to get you into His land of promises.

....

....

....

....

....

....

....

....

....

....

....

....

....

Almighty Lord, because You are with me, I can face anything without fear.

Day 66

A "NEVERTHELESS" GOD

The king and his men went to Jerusalem against the Jebusites, the inhabitants of the land, who said to David, You shall not enter here, for the blind and the lame will prevent you; they thought, David cannot come in here. Nevertheless, David took the stronghold of Zion, that is, the City of David.
2 SAMUEL 5:6–7 AMPC

When the odds appear stacked against you, remember that you have a nevertheless God on your side.

In 2 Samuel 1–5, David, the shepherd boy turned warrior, learns of the deaths of King Saul and Jonathan. After he mourns them both, David asks God where he and his family should go. God tells him to go to Hebron. There David is anointed king of Judah. Afterward a war erupts between the house of David and that of Saul. David comes out victorious and is anointed king of Israel.

King David now turns his eyes to the city of Jebus, which is under the control of the Jebusites. As he and his men stand ready to attack, the Jebusites tell David, " 'You will never get in here. Even the blind and lame can repel you'; thinking, 'David can't get in here' " (2 Samuel 5:6 HCSB). "Nevertheless, David" attacked the city and claimed it as his own, renaming it the City of David, a.k.a. Jerusalem.

No matter what others may say or think, no matter how they may tease or threaten God's people, no matter what words they use against them, God followers can stand firm. For they have in their corner a nevertheless God. They, like David, can become greater and greater because the Lord of hosts is with them (1 Chronicles 11:9).

Believers need just one thing to tap into the power of the nevertheless God: faith. You must believe that no one can defeat your Lord. That you belong to a God "whose power no foe can withstand" (Psalm 91:1 AMPC). You must believe that He will send His angels to aid you, surround you, and deliver you (Psalm 34:7). You must understand that no matter how bad things may look or seem, you are connected to and sheltered by the God who can part seas, annihilate armies, and calm the chaos within and without.

Grow my faith, Lord. Help me to remember that nothing and no one can ever defeat You. For in believing this truth, in putting my confidence in You, I will find calm within and without.

Day 67

THE LORD WHO STAYS

O Lord, you have examined my heart and know everything about me. You know when I sit down or stand up. You know my thoughts even when I'm far away. You see me when I travel and when I rest at home. You know everything I do. You know what I am going to say even before I say it, Lord. You go before me and follow me.
Psalm 139:1–5 NLT

There may be times in your life when you can't seem to find God. When no matter what you do or where you go, His presence seems elusive at best. Those are the times you need to keep your peace, to rest in the knowledge that even though you can't seem to find God, He certainly knows how to find you.

David, through his writing of Psalm 139, informs us that God knows everything that is happening in our lives—within and without. He knows when we rise and when we lie down, when we stay home and when we go out.

Not only does God know the words you speak, but He knows your every thought—every minute of every day! He knows what's going on in your mind and in your heart.

With God in your life, you will never get lost, unless you yourself have cut the cord of communion between you and your heavenly Father. Even then, He'll still know where you are—mentally, spiritually, physically, emotionally, financially. But He'll also know you're not open to His voice. That you're not tapping into His power. That instead of looking for Him, you're hiding or running away from Him.

No matter where you go, God's love will never leave you. His presence will remain with you. So if you're feeling a tad lost, if you can't seem to home in on where God is working in your life, remind yourself that He is helping you. In this very moment. That He is walking with you. That He surrounds you, guiding you with His hand and supporting you with His strength (Psalm 139:10).

God is making you into the person He wants you to be. He's writing a book about your life. Your job is to live it with full faith in and obedience to Him.

Lord, please stay with me. Watch over me. Pour Your love down upon me. Remind me that "when I wake up, you are still with me!" [Psalm 139:18 NLT].

Day 68

GOD'S TRANSFORMATIONAL POWER

"Yet the LORD your God would not listen to Balaam, but He turned the curse into a blessing for you because the LORD your God loves you."
DEUTERONOMY 23:5 HCSB

When Balak was king of Moab, he watched as the Israelites began settling in the plains of Moab. He feared this great influx of God's people. So Balak sent a message to a soothsayer named Balaam, saying:

> *"Look, a people has come out of Egypt; they cover the surface of the land and are living right across from me. Please come and put a curse on these people for me because they are more powerful than I am. I may be able to defeat them and drive them out of the land, for I know that those you bless are blessed and those you curse are cursed." (Numbers 22:5–6 HCSB)*

The elders of Moab and Midian who came with the message to Balaam had money with which to pay his divination fee. After they'd given him their king's request, Balaam told them he'd let them know God's answer the next day.

That night, God told Balaam not to go with the men to curse the Israelites because they were blessed. The next day, Balaam gave Balak's men God's message, which they then relayed to the king.

Balak then sent more powerful and higher-ranking officials to Balaam. Initially, Balaam said that no amount of money could lead him to "go against the command of the LORD my God" (Numbers 22:18 HCSB). But that night,

God told Balaam to go with this second group of men. . .but say and do only what the Lord commanded.

So Balaam went with the second group of Balak's men. But instead of cursing the people of God, the Lord caused Balak to bless them three times (Numbers 23–24).

God makes it clear that no weapon or words formed against His people will ever succeed (Isaiah 54:17). That with Him on the side of His followers, no one can stand against them (Romans 8:31).

Today, take hope and encouragement from these truths. Remember that those with riches and power in the material world have no power against those following God. For He can turn any curse against you into a blessing and any evil against you into good.

Thank You, Lord, for being on my side, for using Your transformational power to turn all evil that comes my way into something good for me and mine!

Day 69

THE POWER OF PERSISTENT PRAYER

[Jesus] told them a parable to the effect that they ought always to pray and not to turn coward (faint, lose heart, and give up).
LUKE 18:1 AMPC

In Luke 18:1–8, Jesus tells His followers a story about how we are to be persistent in prayer. How we are to continue to pray to God no matter how long it takes to receive an answer from Him. How we are never to lose heart or give up coming to the Lord with our requests.

In this parable, Jesus describes a judge who neither feared God nor had any respect for his fellow humans. In the same town where the judge resided and presided was a widow. She kept coming to the judge and asking him to protect her, to defend her, to give her justice against her adversary.

No matter how many times the judge refused her request, the widow kept coming back and pestering him, requesting he help her. Finally, the judge said to himself, "I don't care about what God thinks of me, much less what any mere human thinks. But this widow is driving me crazy. She's never going to quit coming to see me unless I hear her case and provide her legal protection" (Luke 18:4–5 VOICE).

Jesus' point is that if an unjust judge is willing to avenge this persistent petitioner, how much more will God grant justice to His people who call out to Him day and night? Jesus says, "I tell you, He will defend and protect and avenge them speedily" (verse 8 AMPC).

Perhaps you, like this widow, have felt powerless, oppressed, and defenseless in the society in which you live. If so, may you now take up a new kind of hope. May you remember that you have an all-powerful God on your side—one who loves you and wants the best for you. Don't allow yourself to be tempted by anyone or anything to give up going to the Lord, petitioning for your heart's desire. Your prayer will be answered—in His time and in His way!

Lord, sometimes I feel so powerless. I feel as if no matter how much I pray or how much I strive for justice, my pleas go unheard. So here I am before You. You know my cause. You know my request. Please protect and defend me. Bring me justice.

Day 70

THE POWER OF PERSISTENT ACTION

Rizpah daughter of Aiah took sackcloth and spread it for herself on the rock, from the beginning of harvest until rain fell on them, and she did not allow either the birds of the air to come upon them by day or the beasts of the field by night.
2 SAMUEL 21:10 AMPC

Amid a three-year famine, David went to talk with the Lord and ask why he and his people were getting no relief. The Lord told him it was because Saul had threatened and then taken the lives of many of the Gibeonites (a people who had once deceived the Israelites into a vow of peace; see Joshua 9). So David asked the Gibeonites what he could do to make it up to them so that the Lord would bring His people out of the famine.

The Gibeonites wanted none of Saul's treasure. What they did want was seven of Saul's sons to be hanged. King David agreed.

Two of the seven sons of Saul had been birthed by Rizpah, his concubine. Their bodies were hanged with their brothers' bodies on a hill at the beginning of the barley harvest. In extreme grief and dismay, Rizpah "took sackcloth and spread it for herself on the rock, from the beginning of harvest until rain fell on them, and she did not allow either the birds of the air to come upon them by day or the beasts of the field by night" (2 Samuel 21:10 AMPC).

This scene is so heart wrenching that it may have been what inspired Alfred, Lord Tennyson to write:

Flesh of my flesh was gone, but bone of my bone was left—

I stole them all from the lawyers—and you, will you call it a theft?—

My baby, the bones that had suck'd me, the bones that had laughed and had cried—

Theirs? O, no! they are mine—not theirs—they had moved in my side.

Rizpah's persistent action is what finally caught the attention of King David who, when he heard about her, had the bones of Saul and his sons gathered and buried together. "And after that, God heard and answered when His people prayed for the land" (2 Samuel 21:14 AMPC).

May we be motivated to take persistent action because of our love. For when our passion ignites the love of others, we become witnesses of God's great mercy and power.

....

....

....

....

....

....

....

....

....

....

Lord, may my persistent love in action kindle the love in others.

Day 71

NO LINGERING IN THE PAST

The angels hastened Lot, saying, Arise, take thy wife, and thy two daughters, which are here; lest thou be consumed in the iniquity of the city. . . . But his wife looked back from behind him, and she became a pillar of salt. . . . Remember Lot's wife.
GENESIS 19:15, 26; LUKE 17:32 KJV

When Lot and Abraham found the territory they lived in so crowded that their herdsmen were quarreling about whose livestock was whose, Abraham suggested they separate. He gave Lot the choice of land. His nephew chose the well-watered Jordan Valley and moved his tent, pitching it toward Sodom. Before long, Lot was living in Sodom, where "the men. . .were wicked and sinners before the LORD exceedingly" (Genesis 13:13 KJV).

Later, when Abraham learned Sodom was going to be destroyed, he asked God to save the righteous who lived there, even if they only numbered ten. So God sent two angels to Sodom to rescue Lot and his family.

Having become a man of some power within the city limits, Lot met the angels at the gate and asked the strangers to spend the night at his house. Soon he discovered his visitors were not men but angels determined to save him from God's imminent destruction of the city.

The angels told Lot to gather the members of his family. But when Lot went out to speak to his future sons-in-law, they thought he was joking about the city's coming destruction. So at daybreak, the angels urged Lot to get up, take his wife and two daughters, and flee Sodom before they too were wiped out.

At first Lot lingered. But because of God's compassion, the angels grabbed Lot, his wife, and his two daughters by the hand and dragged them out of the city. Once they were safely past the city gates, one of the angels told them, "Run for your lives! Don't look back and don't stop anywhere on the plain! Run to the mountains, or you will be swept away!" (Genesis 19:17 HCSB). As God demolished Sodom and Gomorrah, Lot's wife, lingering in the past, longing for what she'd once had, looked back and became a pillar of salt.

This story reminds us that the past is not a place in which we can live or linger. For our past dissolves steadily behind us.

Never let the panic of the present or fear of the future keep you from moving forward to the place where God leads.

Each day, Lord, help me keep focused on You and where You are guiding me.

BAD TURNINGS

Ahaz took the silver and gold that was found in the house of the Lord, *and in the treasures of the king's house, and sent it for a present to the king of Assyria. And the king of Assyria hearkened unto him. . . . And king Ahaz cut off the borders of the bases, and removed the laver from off them; and took down the sea from off the brasen oxen that were under it, and put it upon the pavement of stones. And the covert for the sabbath that they had built in the house, and the king's entry without, turned he from the house of the* Lord *for the king of Assyria.*
2 Kings 16:8–9, 17–18 KJV

King Ahaz of Judah found himself in a mess of trouble. His city of Jerusalem was being besieged, and instead of turning to God, he turned to Tiglath-pileser, king of Assyria, for help. He identified himself as Tiglath-pileser's servant and son, requesting Tiglath-pileser to save him "out of the hand of the king of Syria, and out of the hand of the king of Israel, which rise up against me" (2 Kings 16:7 KJV).

To sweeten the offer, King Ahaz gave the king of Assyria silver and gold from the Lord's temple and from his own treasury. And Tiglath-pileser accepted the deal.

Later, out of either fear of offending Tiglath-pileser or fear of his seizing them, King Ahaz removed even more riches from the temple. He turned away from God and His dwelling and toward a foreign king. In the end, although Ahaz and his kingdom of Judah did receive relief from their enemies because of King Tiglath-pileser of Assyria, they became his vassals for thirty years.

When we seek help or relief from anyone or anything other than our Lord, we become servants to that person or thing. We then suffer the disastrous consequences of the decision we have made in changing our alliances, depending on someone or something other than the one true and powerful God. About King Ahaz, 2 Chronicles 28:20 (AMPC) tells us, "So Tiglath-pileser king of Assyria came to him and distressed him without strengthening him."

Today, consider ways in which you may have turned away from the Lord and to someone or something else for aid or encouragement—and the results of that turning. Then turn back to the Lord, asking Him for forgiveness while acknowledging that at some point you may suffer the consequences of looking to someone or something other than the Lord.

Forgive me, Lord, for the times I have turned to something or someone other than You for help. In every way, may I keep looking to You alone.

Day 73

THE MIGHTY MITES

"I assure you: This poor widow has put in more than all those giving to the temple treasury. For they all gave out of their surplus, but she out of her poverty has put in everything she possessed—all she had to live on."
MARK 12:43–44 HCSB

In today's verses, Jesus turns His followers' attention to an overlooked, overwrought, and overburdened member of the society in which they lived: the poor widow.

Jesus, in the hearing of all the people, had just told His disciples that they were to beware of the teachers of the religious law because "they shamelessly cheat widows out of their property and then pretend to be pious by making long prayers in public" (Luke 20:47 NLT).

Now Jesus begins watching the people come up to the temple treasury and put in their offerings. He notices the rich men dropping their ample gifts into the offering box. On their heels comes the antithesis of the rich man—a poor widow. She drops in two tiny coins called mites.

After observing the widow's offering, Jesus makes a point of telling His listeners that she has contributed more to God than all the rich men. Why? Because they gave to God out of their "abundance (their surplus); but she has contributed out of her lack and her want, putting in all that she had on which to live" (Luke 21:4 AMPC).

In giving God all that you have, whether it be your money or talents, you're displaying the fact that you trust God to provide for you. You're turning over to Him all that you have and are so that He might do with it, and with you, as He pleases.

Never allow your pride or your fears to get in the way of giving your all to God. When you give in faith and love to the one who holds the world in His hands, you're living the life He has called you to live. For you're following in the footsteps of the one who gave Himself, His all, for you. And because of your attitude of surrender, He will see your loving gift as outweighing anything a rich man could offer.

Lord, I may not have much to offer You. But what I do have—myself, my talents, and my resources—I give You now. In Jesus' name. Amen.

Day 74

STANDING UP

One day a petition was presented by the daughters of Zelophehad—Mahlah, Noah, Hoglah, Milcah, and Tirzah. Their father, Zelophehad, was a descendant of Hepher son of Gilead, son of Makir, son of Manasseh, son of Joseph. These women stood before Moses, Eleazar the priest, the tribal leaders, and the entire community at the entrance of the Tabernacle.
NUMBERS 27:1–2 NLT

Five daughters of a man named Zelophehad were in a predicament. The land was about to be divided up among the people by tribes according to a census. Under the present law they, as women, would have no property rights, neither now nor in the new land that would soon be distributed among the men and their heirs.

So Zelophehad's five daughters—Mahlah, Noah, Hoglah, Milcah, and Tirzah—courageously stood before Moses, the priest Eleazar, the tribal leaders, and all who were congregated at the entrance to the tabernacle and stated their case:

> *Our father died in the wilderness. He was not among those who assembled together against the Lord in the company of Korah, but died for his own sin [as did all those who rebelled at Kadesh], and he had no sons. Why should the name of our father be removed from his family because he had no son? Give to us a possession among our father's brethren. (Numbers 27:3–4 AMPC)*

To his credit, Moses did not simply brush off their concern. Instead, he took it up with God. And God agreed with the five women! He said their claim was justified—that the inheritance of their father should indeed pass on to them!

By standing up for themselves, they found victory not only for their own personal cause but for all the women who would come after them. For the Lord told Moses to tell the Israelites to change the law so that if a man died without a son, his inheritance would go to his daughters; if no daughters, then to his brothers; if no brothers, then to the nearest relative in his clan (verses 8–11).

What a victory! From then on, women would be counted as human beings and legally entitled to the same property rights as men—a precedence that is still considered in legal cases to this very day!

When you see something happening that's not right, stand up and make your voice known. State your case. And God will bring you justice!

Thank You, Lord, for being a God of justice. I pray You would give me the courage to stand up and speak when I see a wrong that should be righted.

Day 75

A TIME TO KEEP SILENCE

To every thing there is a season, and a time to every purpose under the heaven. . .a time to keep silence, and a time to speak.
ECCLESIASTES 3:1, 7 KJV

In our world, our society, our homes, there is a plethora of noise. It comes from the earbuds we wear, the televisions we sit in front of, our computer screens at work and home, our coworkers, our husbands, our children, our pets, and even our cars. More and more news outlets, pundits, and podcasts vie for our attention, telling us what they think we need to know and what they think we should think. It's enough to drive a woman out of her mind.

Yet God reminds us, over and over again, that silence is a good thing for us to experience. That just as there is a time to speak, there is a time for us to be silent. To sit before Him in silent awe. To stop talking, stop listening to the voices of others, and home in on His voice alone.

Psalm 62 gives us some pointers in this regard. David writes, "For God alone my soul waits in silence; from Him comes my salvation. He only is my Rock and my Salvation, my Defense and my Fortress, I shall not be greatly moved" (verses 1–2 AMPC).

Here we are invited to spend some quiet time with God. To settle our soul before Him. To see Him as our steady rock, the one we can depend on in this crazy world and time we live in. Fortressed within His presence, we can experience the peace He wants us to possess, the calm we crave. By experiencing these precious moments of quiet in His presence, we find the strength to remain unmoved within no matter what is happening around us. For our hearts are open to His Word, His voice, His Spirit.

Within this silence, we may speak to our inner being, "My soul, wait only upon God and silently submit to Him" because our "hope and expectation are from Him" (Psalm 62:5 AMPC). We can then remind ourselves once again, "He only is my Rock and my Salvation; He is my Defense and my Fortress, I shall not be moved" (verse 6 AMPC).

There will be times when we will want to and need to pour out our hearts to God (verse 8). But we cannot forget the equal importance of times of silence as we rest in His presence.

Lord, may You fill me with Your peace as I spend some moments before You in silence.

Day 76

SPREAD BEFORE THE LORD

Hezekiah took the letter from the hand of the messengers, read it, then went up to the LORD's temple, and spread it out before the LORD. Then Hezekiah prayed before the LORD.
2 KINGS 19:14–15 HCSB

Hezekiah, king of Judah, received some extremely troubling correspondence from Rabshakeh, a servant of King Sennacherib of Assyria. This foreign enemy was threatening Hezekiah and his people. Even worse, the Assyrian's words mocked the God of all gods. For Rabshakeh had written to King Hezekiah, "Don't let your God, whom you trust, deceive you by promising that Jerusalem will not be handed over to the king of Assyria. Look, you have heard what the kings of Assyria have done to all the countries: they completely destroyed them. Will you be rescued?" (2 Kings 19:10–11 HCSB).

In his heart of hearts, King Hezekiah knew his only help, his only recourse, could be found in Yahweh. So to the Lord he went. And he took with him the letter that mocked his Master.

Once he reached the temple, Hezekiah spread the letter out before the Lord. Then he prayed, first reminding himself of who God was, of the power He held at creation and beyond. He asked God to listen closely to his prayer, to open His eyes and ears. To hear the words the servant of Sennacherib, king of Assyria, had written, mocking Him.

King Hezekiah's final plea was "Now, LORD our God, please save us from his hand so that all the kingdoms of the earth may know that You are the LORD God—You alone" (verse 19 HCSB).

God answered Hezekiah's prayer through the prophet Isaiah, who told him God had heard his prayer and responded with the Lord's words of prophecy against Sennacherib.

That very night "the angel of the LORD went out and struck down 185,000 in the camp of the Assyrians" (verse 35 HCSB). So Sennacherib went home and lived in Nineveh. Then one day, as he was worshipping in the temple of his false god, two of his sons killed him.

When you are in dire need of God's help and presence, don't hesitate to spread a physical representation of your problem before the Lord. It's not that your all-knowing God needs to see or read your source of worry and woe. But it symbolizes the idea that you are placing not just yourself but also what's bothering you in the Lord's hands. Doing so will not only ease your mind but strengthen your faith, increase your fervency in prayer, and kindle the hope that God will answer.

I spread myself and my worries before You, Lord. Hear my prayer!

Day 77

ACCEPTING THE GOOD AND THE BAD

Satan left God and struck Job with terrible sores. Job. . .went and sat on a trash heap, among the ashes. His wife said, "Still holding on to your precious integrity, are you? Curse God and be done with it!" He told her, "You're talking like an empty-headed fool. We take the good days from God—why not also the bad days?"
Job 2:7–10 MSG

Job was living what many would deem a favored life. He had many children, a good source of income, plenty of servants, and robust health. Job was also a man of God.

All those things were put in jeopardy when Satan, the adversary, suggested to God that the only reason Job was so faithful to Him was because God had given him a good life, blessed him with much, and protected him. But if all that was taken away, surely Job would curse Him.

God told Satan, "Behold, all that he has is in your power, only upon the man himself put not forth your hand" (Job 1:12 AMPC). Having been given permission to do his worst to demonstrate to God the frailty of Job's faith, Satan arranged things so that Job lost everything—his kids, riches, and servants—but his health. Although he mourned his losses, he also fell down and worshipped his God, saying, "Naked I came from my mother's womb, naked I'll return to the womb of the earth. God gives, God takes. God's name be ever blessed" (verse 21 MSG).

Satan approached God again, claiming Job would curse the Lord if his health was severely compromised. God once more gave Satan permission to do his worst, except he had to spare Job's life.

Satan then struck Job with painful sores from his head to his toes. "They itched and oozed so badly that he took a piece of broken pottery to scrape himself" (Job 2:8 MSG). As he sat in a heap of ashes, his wife, who did not meet her demise along with their children, advised Job to curse God and die. But he suggested it was only right to take both the good and the bad days from the Lord.

We will have our dark days when others may wonder why we don't just curse God and die. Those may be our days of testing, when we learn to love God not for the gifts He gives us but for Himself.

Your example at Gethsemane teaches me to submit to the Father's will at all costs. Help me do that each and every day, Lord, thanking You for the good while accepting the bad as well.

Day 78

JESUS REVEALED

Jesus let Himself be seen and revealed [Himself] again to the disciples, at the Sea of Tiberias.
JOHN 21:1 AMPC

The disciples had seen and heard the risen Jesus. Perhaps after the second visit from Him in the upper room, the one that finally convinced Thomas that the Lord had indeed been resurrected, they thought they'd seen the last of Him.

Somewhat discouraged and disheartened, as well as missing his close companion, Peter told some fellow disciples he was going fishing, the job he'd had when he first encountered the one who'd vowed to make him a fisher of men. The others agreed to go with him.

The men went out in their boat but caught nothing that night. At daybreak, Jesus stood on the shore. But His followers didn't recognize Him.

Jesus yelled out, "Hey, guys, catch anything?"

"No," the men yelled back.

Then Jesus gave them specific instructions, telling them to cast their nets on the right-hand side of the boat and they'd catch some fish. So they did. And their net was so full they could barely lift it!

That's when John recognized that the man on the shore was Jesus. When Peter heard that, he jumped into the water and swam ashore, leaving the other men to drag in the nets full of fish.

When they got to Jesus, He already had fish cooking over a fire and some bread for them. Together they broke their fast.

When you first encountered Jesus, chances are you were on fire for Him and for the things of God. But then your passion may have cooled somewhat. You even may have become a bit discouraged and disheartened in your faith. Soon you found yourself back to the same old routine. Yet this time seemed different. For you felt like no matter how hard or long you worked, you came up with nothing to show for your efforts. And you wondered where God had gotten to.

If the fire of your faith has cooled somewhat, open your ears and eyes to what is on the shore of your life. For there your Lord stands, waiting and wanting to comfort you. To remind you that He is still there, still working in your life, ready to encourage you and touch your heart through His Spirit.

Jesus wants to guide you in this life, to tell you where to cast your net, where to put your efforts. He wants you to know He is there to help.

Here I am, Lord. Reveal Yourself to me.

Day 79

A MATTER OF HONOR

On the seventh day, when the heart of the king was merry with wine, he commanded Mehuman, Biztha, Harbona, Bigtha, and Abagtha, Zethar, and Carcas, the seven chamberlains that served in the presence of Ahasuerus the king, to bring Vashti the queen before the king with the crown royal, to shew the people and the princes her beauty: for she was fair to look on. But the queen Vashti refused to come at the king's commandment.
ESTHER 1:10–12 KJV

Esther is one of only two Bible books named after a woman, the other being Ruth. Yet before we even meet the title character, we meet another woman. Her name was Vashti, and she was the wife of King Ahasuerus, a.k.a. Xerxes, who ruled from India to Ethiopia.

The king and his queen lived in their palace in Susa, the capital of the Persian Empire. In the third year of King Ahasuerus' reign, he held a feast for all his princes and servants. This event, which was to show off all his riches and excellence, lasted 180 days.

Then the king hosted a party in his garden for all the people who were in his palace. This bash lasted seven days—and the wine was flowing freely. The king had given orders to the wine bearers to serve each person as much as he wanted.

At the same time the king was entertaining the men in the garden, his counterpart Queen Vashti was entertaining the women of the palace inside.

On this seventh day of the king's party, when he was wasted with wine, the king told seven of his personal servants (eunuchs one and all) to bring him his beautiful queen, Vashti, wearing the crown. Ahasuerus wanted to show her off to his guests.

The queen refused to come, perhaps because in the Persian culture, wives, including royal ones, were kept out of the public eye. Whatever her reasoning, Vashti's disobedience angered the king. For if she so publicly disobeyed her husband the king, all wives in the kingdom might follow her example.

Most women know what happens to some men when they've had a bit too much to drink. Overcome with wine, they represent a grave peril for women. Although the consequences of Vashti's refusal cost her the crown, she retained her honor. May we daughters of the King do the same.

Lord, in any sticky situation that arises, give me the strength to retain my honor in Your eyes, no matter what the consequences.

Day 80

THE PROBLEM WITH PRIDE

King Ahasuerus honored Haman. . . . He promoted him in rank and gave him a higher position than all the other officials. The entire royal staff at the King's Gate bowed down and paid homage to Haman, because the king had commanded this to be done for him. But Mordecai would not bow down or pay homage.
ESTHER 3:1–2 HCSB

Once Queen Vashti refused her husband's order, King Ahasuerus removed the crown from her head. Then he increased his harem by rounding up all the pretty young girls in his kingdom. From this bevy of virgins, he would choose his next queen.

Caught in the king's net was a girl named Esther. As an orphan, she'd been given a home by her cousin Mordecai, who adopted her as his daughter. He himself was a Jew who "had been taken into exile from Jerusalem with the other captives when King Nebuchadnezzar of Babylon took King Jeconiah of Judah into exile" (Esther 2:6 HCSB).

When taken into the king's harem, "Esther did not reveal her ethnic background or her birthplace, because Mordecai had ordered her not to" (verse 10 HCSB). Because of her grace and beauty, Esther easily gained favor with those around her and was eventually chosen by Ahasuerus as queen. Even then, she let no one know of her nationality or heritage.

Meanwhile, Haman, Persia's highest-ranking prince and the man closest to King Ahasuerus, often walked by the king's gate where Mordecai sat. Everyone inside and outside the palace would bow when Haman walked by—everyone but Mordecai. This apparent insubordination caused Haman to seethe with rage.

When Haman discovered Mordecai was a Jew, he came up with a plan to kill not just Mordecai but all Jews in Ahasuerus' entire kingdom. He had lots "cast before him day after day [to find a lucky day for his venture]" (Esther 3:7 AMPC).

Once a date was fixed for his holocaust, Haman spoke lies into the king's ear, telling him that the Jews throughout his kingdom were different than all other people, as were their laws. Because they didn't abide by the king's laws, said Haman, these Jews should be exterminated. When the king signed Haman's prepared edict, every Jew's life was in jeopardy.

One man's wounded pride can generate an amazing amount of evil. Proverbs tells us, "GOD can't stomach arrogance or pretense; believe me, he'll put those braggarts in their place. . . . First pride, then the crash—the bigger the ego, the harder the fall" (16:5, 18 MSG).

May we reserve our allegiance and obeisance for God alone, and let the prideful fall where they may.

Lord, may I bow to You alone.

Day 81

IT BEARS REPEATING

As I was with Moses, so I will be with you; I will not fail you or forsake you. Be strong (confident) and of good courage. . . . Only you be strong and very courageous. . . . Have not I commanded you? Be strong, vigorous, and very courageous. Be not afraid, neither be dismayed, for the Lord your God is with you wherever you go.
JOSHUA 1:5–7, 9 AMPC

This message that God imparts to Joshua, the leader of His people after Moses' death, bears repeating and applying.

The Lord begins with a promise to Joshua, saying that wherever he walks, wherever the soles of his feet touch down, is already his for the taking. Then He begins encouraging Joshua by telling him that no one will be able to stand against him (Joshua 1:5). That He will be with him, just as He was with Moses. That He will neither leave nor forsake him.

Then the Lord tells Joshua the first of His three be-strong-and-courageous commands. God needs Joshua to embody these attributes, to take them to heart and embed them in his spirit, mind, and soul. To continually repeat them to himself so that he doesn't fail in his mission: to bring God's people into the Promised Land.

Only by believing that God is with him, imbuing him with all the strength and courage he needs, will Joshua be able to do all that Moses commanded him to do, to follow Moses' instructions to the letter, turning to neither the right nor the left. Only then will he be successful in his endeavors for the Lord God (verse 8).

The instructions from Moses made up the "Book of the Law" God had given him (verse 8). This book is what Joshua was to drench himself with so that it permeated every part of his being. In this way, God's Word would inform everything he thought and every decision he made. The Lord leaves Joshua with one more command to be strong and very courageous and to resist panicking. For with the law within him and God beside him, there was no way he would fail.

You too are to be strong and courageous in your journey with the Lord. To remember that He is right beside you. To make His Book, His Word, His Son, His Spirit an essential and integral part of your being. Only then will you experience true success as you enter His land of promise.

Thank You, Lord, for this essential reminder of what I am to do and how I am to be!

Day 82

THE POWER AWAITS

Inside the city, near the Sheep Gate, was the pool of Bethesda, with five covered porches. Crowds of sick people—blind, lame, or paralyzed—lay on the porches. One of the men lying there had been sick for thirty-eight years.
JOHN 5:2–5 NLT

There are the people lying upon the banks beside the power of God. They're weak, tired persons, trying to live this life in their own strength. They're so feeble because of their misgivings, misdoings, and misthinking that they can barely work up the strength to find help. They're blind, ignorant to all that is spiritual, deaf to the words of God, too frozen to consider good works, simply limping or, even worse, crawling through life as best they can. Too debilitated even to ask for help at times.

The not-quite-whole people lying by the pool of Bethesda were watching the water, apparently waiting for it to begin to ripple, for it was said that at certain times an angel stirred up those waters. Whoever then first stepped into the water would be healed.

God knows about these languishing people. They're the ones Jesus' heart goes out to, the ones who, unbeknownst to them, are waiting for the Spirit's touch.

Such a person lying near Bethesda's pool was a man who, as Jesus already knew, had been sick for thirty-eight years. To this man, Jesus asked a simple question: "Do you want to become well? [Are you really in earnest about getting well?]" (John 5:6 AMPC).

The man didn't answer this question with an unequivocal yes or no. Instead, he offered Jesus an explanation of why he could not get himself well, saying, "Sir, I have nobody when the water is moving to put me into the pool; but while I am trying to come [into it] myself, somebody else steps down ahead of me" (verse 7 AMPC).

Jesus, seeing this man had no one in his life to aid him in his search for healing, knew his heart was open to receiving a gift of healing, of wholeness, of life. The man's helplessness summoned Jesus' power of love, healing, and strength. As Jesus spoke, He knew the man was being healed, that His energy flowing out of Him had already warmed the eyes of the expectant face before Him. So He simply said, "Stand up, pick up your mat, and walk!" (verse 8 NLT). The man, instantly healed, rolled up his sleeping mat and began walking away!

If you yourself are feeling incomplete, alone, sick at heart, or soul weary, open yourself to the power of Christ that awaits you. Then rise up and walk!

Lord, make me whole!

Day 83

ETERNAL LIFE

The person whose ears are open to My words [who listens to My message] and believes and trusts in and clings to and relies on Him Who sent Me has (possesses now) eternal life. And he does not come into judgment [does not incur sentence of judgment, will not come under condemnation], but he has already passed over out of death into life.

JOHN 5:24 AMPC

Jesus is telling His listeners, those who hear with their hearts, that if they are open to and believe His message, the words He says; if they trust in, hang on to, and rely on God the Father of all, they even now possess eternal life!

"Passing over" out of death (the life you were living) and into life (the one you now have in Jesus) was something you did of your own accord. It wasn't anything anyone forced or coerced you to do. It was something your heart led you into when you willingly and gratefully agreed to accept Christ's sacrifice on your behalf.

You no longer need to worry about the life you once lived. Nor do you need to worry about whether (and when) you'll make it to heaven. You are already in that eternal time zone. Each and every day of this new life, you are getting to know more and more about Jesus, what He says, what His words mean, who His Father (and yours) is.

You no longer need to fear death. You are already living and walking, breathing and talking with the Son of God who cleared the pathway for you, the Father who has always loved you, and the Spirit who is there to comfort, love, guide, and translate for you.

You no longer need to fear anything or anyone you may encounter along the way, along the course Jesus has set you upon. You need not hesitate to follow Jesus' guidance, to step out of your comfort zone, to take on a task you might have veered away from before, because you are already with your eternal strength, companion, refuge, and rock.

Once you realize this miraculous gift you have been given, chances are you'll want to tell other people about it. And the best way to do that is to live as Jesus did—to live unfettered from worldly wants and charms; to love all, especially the seemingly unlovable; to give without asking anything in return; to serve regardless of race, creed, religion, color; and to tap into the peace of God in the midst of chaos. In other words, to live the eternal life you've been given.

Help me forever live as You lived, Lord.

Day 84

ADRIFT

"I will never again cause the feet of the Israelites to wander from the land I gave to their ancestors if only they will be careful to do all I have commanded them. . . ." But they did not listen; Manasseh caused them to stray so that they did greater evil than the nations the Lord *had destroyed before the Israelites.*
2 Kings 21:8–9 HCSB

God tried to get His people living in Judah to listen to Him, to obey the laws He'd given them through Moses. But they refused to listen. And so did their king. As a result, they committed more acts of evil than the nations God had destroyed in His Promised Land!

Why did His people stray so far from Him and His laws? Because they had lost the book of His law! (See 2 Kings 22:8–13.) How could they follow the rules that had not seen the light of day in such a long time?

When people don't have a rule book or a worthy leader to get behind, they often do one of two things. The first is to make up their own rules. The second is to follow the rules of the people they live beside. Thus, instead of following the one true God, the people living in the Promised Land were following Baal and Asherah (2 Kings 23:4), Molech (verse 10), Ashtoreth, Chemosh, and Milcom (verse 13).

Baal was a fertility god, the worship of whom involved sex orgies. Asherah was a mother goddess, associated with sacred trees.

Molech was a god honored by the sacrifice of children who were forced to pass through or into fire. He was revered as a protecting father. Leviticus strictly forbade God's people to worship this false idol (18:21; 20:1–5), who later was honored by both kings Solomon and Manasseh.

Ashtoreth was a goddess of fertility who was identified with the planet Venus. She played dual roles, being the patroness of not only war but also sex. Solomon and God's people succumbed to her charms as well.

Chemosh, the deity of the Moabites, also had children sacrificed to her through fire. Solomon's altar to her in Jerusalem was not destroyed until King Josiah's purge (2 Kings 22–23). And finally, Milcom was another god Solomon worshipped and Josiah brought down.

The further God's people drifted from the words of the one true God, the more their hearts turned to other gods. Today, consider where you might be turning for truth and comfort. Then pray that God would help you find your way back to Him and His Word.

Help me not to stray from
You and Your Word, Lord!

Day 85

ALL IN

"The most important commandment is this: 'Listen, O Israel! The Lord our God is the one and only Lord. And you must love the Lord your God with all your heart, all your soul, all your mind, and all your strength.' The second is equally important: 'Love your neighbor as yourself.' No other commandment is greater than these."
Mark 12:29–31 NLT

When Jesus gave His followers these two commandments, they were not anything new to God's people. For Moses had written, "The Lord is our God, the Lord alone. And you must love the Lord your God with all your heart, all your soul, and all your strength" in Deuteronomy 6:4–5 (NLT). And "Do not seek revenge or bear a grudge against a fellow Israelite, but love your neighbor as yourself" in Leviticus 19:18 (NLT).

Thus, since the earliest days of wilderness wanderings, then into the days of the judges and kings, the people were aware of what God had commanded them. But the kings who followed these two greatest commandments were few and far between. One of the last truly good kings over God's people was King Josiah of Judah, "who turned to the Lord with all his heart and soul and strength, obeying all the laws of Moses. And there has never been a king like him since" (2 Kings 23:25 NLT).

In the eighteenth year of his reign, Josiah began looking into temple repairs. There the book of the law was discovered (2 Kings 22:8–10). When the book was read to him, Josiah tore his clothes in despair. Later he demanded it be read from beginning to end to all the people. King Josiah then and there "pledged to obey the Lord by keeping all his commands, laws, and decrees with all his heart and soul" (2 Kings 23:3 NLT). After making that vow to God, Josiah began to make reforms by purging all the foreign gods in his territory and in the temple of the Lord itself!

Sometimes we too can become lax in our attention to, worship of, and obedience to God. We too may need to make some reforms, to purge our lives and homes, as well as our hearts, souls, and minds, of people or things that have become our idols or false gods. We too may need to turn back to the beginning, when we first started to follow God faithfully, and make sure we are all in with Him.

Show me, Lord, what I need to purge from my life so that You alone will be my King, Master, and God.

Day 86

KNOWN

Jesus saw Nathanael coming toward Him and said about him, "Here is a true Israelite; no deceit is in him." "How do you know me?" Nathanael asked. "Before Philip called you, when you were under the fig tree, I saw you," Jesus answered. "Rabbi," Nathanael replied, "You are the Son of God! You are the King of Israel!"

JOHN 1:47–49 HCSB

One day Jesus decided to head to Galilee. He found Philip and told him to follow Him. Philip then found Nathanael and said to him, "We have found the One Moses wrote about in the Law (and so did the prophets): Jesus the son of Joseph, from Nazareth!" (John 1:45 HCSB).

When Nathanael asked if anything good could come out of that town, Philip answered with "Come and see" (verse 46 HCSB). So Nathanael did.

When Nathanael came nearer to Jesus, He described Nathanael's character aloud, saying, "Here is an Israelite indeed [a true descendant of Jacob], in whom there is no guile nor deceit nor falsehood nor duplicity!" (verse 47 AMPC).

Having never met Jesus before, Nathanael asked how Jesus knew him. Bible scholars have surmised that Jesus must have seen Nathanael sitting under the fig tree in his garden. That's where Nathanael was when Philip went to tell him about Jesus.

Jews would often seek the silence and solace of God in a private place, in a grove or garden, under the shade of a tree, where they could meditate and pray in the stillness of the day. As Nathanael met with God, he may have been praying fervently for direction, for comfort, for truth, for peace. Jesus, the one who knows the secrets of our hearts, the one with whom we commune, the one who speaks in the ears of holy angels, sending them to help and shield us, already knew Nathanael from the inside out. That's how Jesus could speak with knowledge about the man He'd never physically encountered until that moment in time.

Jesus, the Son of God our Father, sees you in those private times of prayer, even though you may not, in those moments, consider Him coming into your space. He hears what you say in those secret meetings with Him. And from those moments in time, He draws conclusions about your character. At the same time, you might know very little about His (see John 14:9).

Today, as you enter your private place of prayer, experience the divine intimacy of meeting with the one you love, the one who sees, knows, and loves you like no other. Get to know Him like He knows you.

....

....

....

....

....

....

....

....

....

....

....

....

Lord, meet me in this quiet place of prayer.

Day 87

THE APPROVAL OF ONE

That's why it is hard to see how true faith is even possible for you: you are consumed by the approval of other men, longing to look good in their eyes; and yet you disregard the approval of the one true God.
JOHN 5:44 VOICE

When the kingdom of Judah was attacked and conquered by the Babylonians, King Nebuchadnezzar brought back to Babylon not just some of the treasures from God's temple but many of God's own children as well. Some of these captive Israelites were young men of noble birth, handsome as well as wise. Nebuchadnezzar's idea was to make them servants of his court after they had completed three years of training.

Among these young nobles were Daniel, Hananiah, Mishael, and Azariah of Judah. Once in Babylon, they each underwent a name change: "Belteshazzar to Daniel, Shadrach to Hananiah, Meshach to Mishael, and Abednego to Azariah" (Daniel 1:7 HCSB).

These young men were put under the charge of the chief of the eunuchs, who wanted to serve them rich food and wine. "But Daniel was determined not to defile himself by eating the food and wine given to them by the king" (verse 8 NLT). So Daniel asked the head eunuch if he could eat only the food that would be acceptable to God, food not tainted by having been an offering to an idol.

Apparently, fear of losing his head prompted the chief eunuch, whom God had moved to favor Daniel, to say, "My lord the king assigned your food and drink. I'm afraid of what would happen if he saw your faces looking thinner than those of the other young men your age. You would endanger my life with the king" (verse 10 HCSB).

So Daniel suggested that perhaps the chief could serve Daniel and his three companions nothing but vegetables and water for ten days. Then he could compare their appearance with that of those who'd been eating the king's food and base his final decision on what he saw. The chief agreed. At the end of the ten days, Daniel, Hananiah, Mishael, and Azariah all looked healthier than the other young men who'd been eating the king's food! So their vegetarian diet sans wine continued!

As a reward for their faithfulness, God gave these four young men much wisdom, knowledge, and learning. And Daniel was given the special ability to interpret dreams and visions.

May you too seek and find approval in the eyes of only one!

Lord, may I develop true faith by desiring approval from You alone!

Day 88

AGENDAS

All that My Father gives to Me comes to Me. . . . And here's the reason: I have come down from heaven not to pursue My own agenda but to do what He desires. I am here on behalf of the Father who sent Me.
JOHN 6:37–38 VOICE

Just as God had a plan for His Son, He has a plan for you. And this plan is to be your top priority. You're to have no other agenda but to do what He has called you to do, to live as He has called you to live. For God tells His people through the prophet Jeremiah:

> *I know the thoughts and plans that I have for you, says the Lord, thoughts and plans for welfare and peace and not for evil, to give you hope in your final outcome. Then you will call upon Me, and you will come and pray to Me, and I will hear and heed you. Then you will seek Me, inquire for, and require Me [as a vital necessity] and find Me when you search for Me with all your heart. I will be found by you, says the Lord. (Jeremiah 29:11–14 AMPC)*

So how do you determine the plan God has for you? How do you figure out what your holy agenda is? You turn yourself, your entire self—mind, body, soul, and spirit—over to God. You remind yourself daily that nothing is impossible for Him. That you can do whatever He has called you to do. That He will give you everything you need to accomplish His purposes for you.

Open your mind to the Lord. Open your heart to His Spirit. Listen for His voice in His promises, His love, His light. Keep in mind the power of God's Word—how it is what He used to form the world, the cosmos, the chair you're sitting on, the bed you lie upon at night, the grass at your feet, the roof over your head, the book you hold in your hand.

Know that He is the one who commands the earth, spreading the snow like wool, frost like ashes. "He throws His hailstones like crumbs. Who can withstand His cold? He sends His word and melts them; He unleashes His winds, and the waters flow" (Psalm 147:17–18 HCSB).

Today, seek God's face and voice. Feel His power. Immerse yourself in His Word. And make His agenda yours.

May I live my life as You desire, Lord.

Day 89

RESOLVED TO FOLLOW

It has come to our attention that certain Jews whom you appointed to govern in the province of Babylon are ignoring your order, O king. They refuse to serve your gods, our gods, and they do not fall and worship the golden statue you erected. Their names: Shadrach, Meshach, and Abed-nego.
DANIEL 3:12 VOICE

King Nebuchadnezzar of Babylon had made a gold statue ninety feet high. Upon its erection, he sent a herald to proclaim that people from every nation and language were to fall down and worship this statue whenever they heard playing "every kind of music" (Daniel 3:5 HCSB). Those who would not fall down and worship the idol would be thrown into a fiery furnace.

So pretty much everyone of every nation and language fell down and worshipped the statue when the music played. Well, everyone except some Jews who'd been captured by the Babylonians, namely, Shadrach, Meshach, and Abednego. Consequently, some men of Chaldean descent went to their king and told him about these three young Jews.

Nebuchadnezzar flew into a rage at the thought that someone would disobey his mandate. So he sent for Shadrach, Meshach, and Abednego. He asked if the accusations against them were true, reminding them what the consequences of their disobedience would be.

They replied, "If the God we serve exists, then He can rescue us from the furnace of blazing fire, and He can rescue us from the power of you, the king. But even if He does not rescue us, we want you as king to know that we will not serve your gods or worship the gold statue you set up" (verses 17–18 HCSB).

Now even more infuriated, the king had the temperature of the furnace raised seven times hotter than normal. He commanded some soldiers to tie up the three Jews and throw them into the fire.

Because of the extreme heat, the soldiers were killed immediately. But not the bound Jews. For when Nebuchadnezzar looked into the furnace, he saw "four men, not tied, walking around in the fire unharmed; and the fourth looks like a son of the gods" (verse 25 HCSB).

The king commanded the Jews to come out. When they did, not one thread of clothing nor one hair on their heads was singed. They didn't even smell of smoke!

When you resolve to follow the one and only true God, when you refuse to succumb to the idols of this earth, when you live a life of love and obedience to God and compassion toward others regardless of the earthly consequences, you too will be protected. For then you'll be in step with the Son of God.

I resolve to follow You, Lord, wherever You lead me in love.

Day 90

UNDETERRED IN FAITH

"All the administrators of the kingdom, the prefects, satraps, advisers, and governors have agreed that the king should establish an ordinance and enforce an edict that for 30 days, anyone who petitions any god or man except you, the king, will be thrown into the lions' den. . . ." So King Darius signed the document.
DANIEL 6:7, 9 HCSB

Over his 120 provinces, King Darius assigned high officers. Over the officers, he assigned three administrators, one of whom was Daniel, an exile from Judah.

Because of Daniel's wisdom and good spirit, Darius decided to place him over his entire realm. This promotion very much dismayed and discomforted the leaders under Daniel, so they began to watch for any fault in Daniel or his actions.

Knowing Daniel prayed to the God of Israel three times a day, these jealous leaders came up with a scheme to do away with Daniel. They talked the king into signing a law saying that those who worshipped anyone but him would be tossed into the lions' den. Darius agreed.

Even though Daniel knew this law had been put into effect, "he went home and. . .prayed three times a day, just as he had always done, giving thanks to his God" (Daniel 6:10 NLT).

When the ne'er-do-wells gleefully discovered Daniel continuing to worship his God as he'd always done, they ran to tell the king. Although Darius, who liked Daniel, was deeply disturbed about the trap Daniel had fallen into, he saw no way out of it. With a heavy heart, King Darius ordered Daniel arrested and thrown into the lions' den, saying, "May your God, whom you serve so faithfully, rescue you" (verse 16 NLT).

After a sleepless night, the king ran down to the lions' den. He called out, "Daniel, servant of the living God! Was your God, whom you serve so faithfully, able to rescue you from the lions?" (verse 20 NLT). Darius heard Daniel reply, "My God sent his angel to shut the lions' mouths so that they would not hurt me, for I have been found innocent in his sight. And I have not wronged you, Your Majesty" (verse 22 NLT).

Not a scratch was found on Daniel because he had trusted in God (verse 23). On the contrary, the men who'd maliciously accused Daniel of acting against the king, as well as their families, were ravaged by the lions before their bodies hit the floor of the den.

Never doubt the protection of your living God.

Thank You, Lord, for keeping Your faithful ones safe in the palm of Your hand.

Day 91

A WOMAN OF INFLUENCE

Make the things I'm commanding you today part of who you are. Repeat them to your children. Talk about them when you're sitting together in your home and when you're walking together down the road. Make them the last thing you talk about before you go to bed and the first thing you talk about the next morning.
DEUTERONOMY 6:6–7 VOICE

A barren Hannah had prayed to God, asking for a child. If He granted this request, Hannah promised to dedicate that child to the Lord (1 Samuel 1). When she finally conceived and gave birth to her son Samuel, Hannah knew her time with him was limited. For she had determined to take him to live and serve in the house of God once he was weaned.

Bible scholars estimate that Samuel was weaned when he was two to four years old. That was Hannah's only window of opportunity to love her baby and teach him about the Lord so that he would be of use to God's servants when he went to live at the tabernacle of the Lord. (Amazingly enough, today's experts agree that the most critical time of a child's development is between birth and the age of three or five years old!)

Hannah must've done an excellent job not just teaching her boy Samuel about God but also showing him how to be a good and loyal God follower, for Samuel eventually became a major player in God's plans. He became not only a faithful follower of God but a prophet, a priest, and a judge!

A thousand years after Samuel, the apostle Paul wrote to his spiritual son Timothy, "What strikes me most is how natural and sincere your faith is. I am convinced that the same faith that dwelt in your grandmother, Lois, and your mother, Eunice, abides in you as well" (2 Timothy 1:5 VOICE).

Here we have another example of the spiritual influence a woman can have on a child's life.

Studies continue to show that mothers have the most influence over their children. Yet whether that child is natural born, adopted, fostered, a grandchild, a niece or nephew, a neighbor, or a Sunday school attendee, you too can help to shape their faith—which is just what God has commanded His followers to do.

Today, consider the children in your own life. Think about ways you can influence them for God by relating His Word to them or setting a godly example, thereby shedding God's light into their lives.

Lord, make me a woman of influence in a child's life. Help me to connect a little one with You, to boost their faith, to enable their to know and love You.

Day 92

FINDING A VOICE

"If you stay silent during this time, deliverance for the Jews will come from somewhere, but you, my child, and all of your father's family will die. And who knows? Perhaps you have been made queen for such a time as this."
ESTHER 4:14 VOICE

When Esther's cousin and adoptive father Mordecai learned of the wicked plot hatched by Haman to exterminate the Jews in the kingdom of Persia, he ripped the clothes he was wearing, donned sackcloth, and wiped ashes upon himself. He then went through the city weeping aloud. Finally, nearing the king's gate, he stopped.

When Queen Esther heard about Mordecai's behavior, she gave some servants clothes to take to him. But he refused to wear them. Esther then sent out her servant Hathach to find out what the matter was. Mordecai told the servant about Haman's plot to destroy the Jews. He even gave Hathach a copy of the order that had been sent to all the provinces. And he told the servant to "convince [Esther] to go before her king and plead for his favor, not only for her life, but also for the lives of her people" (Esther 4:8 VOICE).

After receiving this information, Esther sent word back to Mordecai, asking him how she was supposed to see the king. If she came into his presence without being invited, she could be put to death!

Mordecai responded by telling her that if she stayed quiet now, someone else would save the Jews, but she and all her family (perhaps Mordecai himself) might die in the meantime. Then he said, "Perhaps you have been made queen for such a time as this."

Although God's name is never mentioned in the book of Esther, He is clearly working behind the scenes to bring about the deliverance of His exiled people. And Esther was meant to play a crucial role in that deliverance.

In the end, after much prayer and fasting among the queen's maids and the Jewish people in the city, Esther did indeed seek an audience with the king. Drawing on her God-given courage and voice, she played her part in saving her people.

Today, consider the various ways God is working in your life and where you may need to garner courage to be a part of God's plan. Consider that perhaps you are here now for such a time as this.

What is Your plan for me, Lord, in this time and place?

Day 93

PERFECT TIMING

The course of my life is in Your power; deliver me from the power of my enemies and from my persecutors.
PSALM 31:15 HCSB

Esther had decided to put her life on the line by seeking an uninvited audience with the king, telling Mordecai, "If I perish, I perish" (Esther 4:16 HCSB). She would go before the king only after three days of prayer and fasting by her maids and the Jews within the fortress city of Susa.

Fortunately, instead of having Esther killed for seeking his presence without first receiving an invitation, the king was delighted to see her. In fact, Ahasuerus said, "What is it, Queen Esther? What is your request? I'll give you anything—even half of my kingdom—all you need to do is ask" (Esther 5:3 VOICE).

Esther responded by requesting the king and his right-hand man Haman to attend a banquet in their honor. The king readily accepted, and both he and Haman showed up to Esther's feast.

There the king once again asked Esther her request, with the same sort of kingdom-offering speech. Instead of revealing her nationality as a Jew and asking her king and husband to rescind his decree (inspired by Haman) to have all her brethren and herself killed in a mass extermination, Esther asked Ahasuerus and Haman to attend another banquet the next day.

No reason is given for why Esther delayed revealing her nationality and asking her king to spare herself and her people. Perhaps she thought both men needed more flattery and wine before she stated her case. Whatever the reason, with so many lives hanging in the balance, Esther bided her time.

And because she did so, God worked things so that when the king retired to his room shortly after the first banquet, he was sleepless. Hoping to be put asleep by his servant's droning voice, Ahasuerus requested that his history be read to him. It was then he was reminded of how Mordecai saved him from an assassination attempt and was not rewarded for it.

While King Ahasuerus was figuring out some way to honor Mordecai, Haman was figuring out how to kill Mordecai before the rest of his countrymen were exterminated.

Both Esther and Mordecai recognized that God held their lives in His hands. That He would be faithful to work out His plans according to His timetable. And that within His will was the safest place they could be. May all God followers do the same.

I bow to Your wisdom, Lord, and bide my time, knowing Your timing is perfect.

Day 94

EVIL GETS ITS DUES

The wicked conceive evil; they are pregnant with trouble and give birth to lies. They dig a deep pit to trap others, then fall into it themselves.
PSALM 7:14–15 NLT

The nose of Haman, King Ahasuerus' right-hand man, was put out of joint because Mordecai the Jew would not bow to him. So Haman had an edict drafted to exterminate all the Jews throughout the Persian Empire on a particular day. After Ahasuerus signed the edict into law, Haman made sure the proclamation was delivered to every province throughout the kingdom. Little did Haman know he was going to fall into his own trap.

Haman was delighted to be at the queen's first banquet. And when Esther invited him and the king to another feast the next evening, Haman was beside himself!

Full of joy, he began his journey home from the palace. But his gleefulness spiraled and his rage spiked when he saw Mordecai at the gate, "unwilling to stand and, worse still, seemingly unafraid" (Esther 5:9 VOICE). To his credit, Haman held in his anger and continued his journey home.

In the presence of his family and company, Haman bragged about his wealth, his status, his closeness to the king, and his second invitation to dine with him and the queen. The only thing that continued to grind his gears was Mordecai.

To bring the roses back into his cheeks, Haman's friends and family encouraged him to build a gallows on which to hang Mordecai the very next day! Haman, overjoyed at this idea, authorized the building to begin immediately!

Yet the next day, the king decided that Mordecai was to be honored.

Ironically, as the king pondered how to publicly laud the man he wanted to honor, Haman wrongly guessed he was the one the king desired to distinguish above all others! As it turned out, Haman was the one who had to seat Mordecai on a horse. A horse Haman himself then had to lead around the city, parading Mordecai around and proclaiming, "This is what is done for the man the king wants to honor" (Esther 6:9 HCSB).

Fortunately, Haman had the second banquet to look forward to that evening. But there the queen revealed that she was a Jew. In the end, Haman himself was hanged on the gallows he had built for Mordecai.

This story reminds us not to waste time and energy worrying about or fearing those who do evil. For God will work things out so that the wicked who build a trap for others will fall into it themselves!

....

....

....

....

....

....

....

....

....

....

....

....

I'm free of worry and fear, Lord, for I know You'll ensure that those who are evil get their just dues.

Day 95

OUTSIDE THE BOX

Now to Him Who, by (in consequence of) the [action of His] power that is at work within us, is able to [carry out His purpose and] do superabundantly, far over and above all that we [dare] ask or think [infinitely beyond our highest prayers, desires, thoughts, hopes, or dreams]—to Him be glory.
EPHESIANS 3:20–21 AMPC

God often works out His plans in ways that are outside the box. There are times when He flaunts customs and traditions, does the unexpected, goes beyond what we'd ever thought, hoped, or imagined.

God uses Rahab, a prostitute, to hide Joshua's spies from the authorities who wanted to kill them. She then rides off with the vanquishing Israelites and becomes an ancestor of Jesus!

In a day when women are not considered reliable witnesses, God makes Mary Magdalene the first person to see the resurrected Jesus and the first messenger to spread the Good News!

God enlists Moses, a murderer with a lisp, to go before Pharaoh of Egypt and speak for His people. Later, when God sends His Son to earth, He has Him enter the world not as a strong and mighty warrior but as a helpless babe. Born not in a castle to wealthy parents but in a stable to a couple of humble means.

God turns Saul, a hardworking persecutor of Christians, into Paul, an avid and faithful follower of Christ who goes on to author many of the New Testament letters.

God uses Gideon, a man whose family is the weakest in his tribe and he the youngest in his family, to become a mighty warrior and save His people.

Whatever your problem, predicament, or plea, believe that God will, in His own way and time, come up with the perfect solution. Be assured that His wisdom is beyond your comprehension. Remember that He can see every side of each situation. As a result, you can leave everything in His more than capable hands.

Just keep in mind that God, who continually thinks outside the box, is the one to whom we are to entrust our woes and worries. For even while we try to work out what might be possible, He's busy putting events into motion, calling people, performing feats, and bringing solutions into play in a way that exceeds our comprehension and the realm of possibility.

I willingly and gratefully leave myself, my plans, my expectations, and all my concerns in Your hands, Lord.

Day 96

CATCHING YOUR BREATH

You have six days to work. When the seventh day arrives, stop all work so that your ox and donkey can rest. When you observe the Sabbath Day, your female slave's son and any outsider serving you have a chance to catch their breath and relax.
EXODUS 23:12 VOICE

In the very beginning, God brought humans to life with His breath (Genesis 2:7). Ever since then, God has reminded us, day after day, that we need to rest, to stop and catch that breath of His Spirit, to relax and spend some time dwelling on Him and His labor of love in our lives.

For some reason, many are resistant to taking time to rest or simply find it difficult to do so. Perhaps one obstacle is that so many of us are working hard, burning the candle at both ends, trying to keep our heads above water, our families afloat. In those situations, breathers are few and far between.

Another obstacle to the rest we need is the constant news reported through newspaper headlines, magazines, online sources, radio, and television screens. Because outlets tend to highlight bad news over good, we may find ourselves wide awake until the wee hours as we worry about what might happen next and what effect it could have on our family.

It doesn't help that we've recently been hit with outbreaks of war, terrorism plots, lethal pandemics, wallet-denting recessions, and back-biting politics. As our very lives are overturned, we wonder if we'll ever get back to normal.

Meanwhile, God. Our unchanging Creator continues to remind us to take a rest, to catch the breath that He gave us at the beginning of our lives and will take away at the end of our time here on earth. For only with His much-needed regeneration will we find the strength, power, calm, and clarity that we need to do what God has called His daughters to do. To stand firm. To find the calm and hope within each storm. To witness the rainbow after the flood.

Find some time each day to catch your breath. In that moment of stillness, allow Jesus to breathe His Spirit and peace into your heart (John 20:21–22) and provide comfort, mending, and rejuvenation where needed (Psalm 34:18).

"God, my shepherd! I don't need a thing.
You have bedded me down in lush meadows,
you find me quiet pools to drink from.
True to your word, you let me catch
my breath and send me in the right
direction" [Psalm 23:1–3 MSG].

Day 97

FULL COMMITMENT

She said, I will surely go with you; nevertheless, the trip you take will not be for your glory, for the Lord will sell Sisera into the hand of a woman. And Deborah arose and went with Barak.
JUDGES 4:9 AMPC

In the days of the judges, God raised up two women to save His people.

Deborah was a wife, a prophet, and a judge who would sit beneath a palm tree and settle arguments people had with one another.

This was during the days when Jabin, the king of Canaan, ruled. His general, a man named Sisera, had nine hundred iron chariots that he used to abuse the Israelites for twenty years. When His people began to cry out for help, God sent Deborah a message for an Israelite military leader named Barak.

Barak visited Deborah at her request. She told him that God wanted him to travel to Mount Tabor with ten thousand soldiers. God's plan was to draw Sisera's forces (with nine hundred chariots) to meet Barak's troops at the Kishon River. There God would bring victory to Israel.

Barak refused to take on this assignment unless Deborah went with him, saying, "If you won't go with me, then I won't go either." Deborah agreed to go with him but warned that because he wasn't fully committed to God and His plan, the glory for this victory would go to a woman.

As Barak and Deborah faced Sisera's forces together, everything happened just as God had said it would. He confused the chariot drivers and all of King Jabin's fighting men. And every man died by the sword except Sisera, their commander, who fled on foot.

Running to the tent of Heber the Kenite, Sisera thought "himself safe at last, since there was peace between Jabin, the king of Hazor, and Heber the Kenite" (Judges 4:17 VOICE). But Sisera hadn't counted on Jael, the wife of Heber.

Jael invited Sisera into her tent, telling him he had nothing to fear there. Once he was inside, Jael covered Sisera with a rug in case Barak's soldiers came looking for him. She then gave him a little milk to drink. After he fell asleep, Jael "took a tent peg in one hand and a hammer in the other. She crept softly to his side. Then she drove the peg into his temple, down into the ground, and killed him" (verse 21 VOICE).

God brings victory to those who are fully committed to Him. Do you meet that description? If so, just imagine what God will do through you!

Lord, may I have the courage and faith to be a woman fully committed to You.

Day 98

CONSIDER THE LILIES

Consider the lilies of the field and learn thoroughly how they grow; they neither toil nor spin. . . . If God so clothes the grass of the field, which today is alive and green and tomorrow is tossed into the furnace, will He not much more surely clothe you, O you of little faith?
MATTHEW 6:28, 30 AMPC

Everything we see, hear, touch, smell, and taste in nature has a trace of its Creator within it. To get to know God better, to grow closer to Him and begin to understand Him more, we need to take the time to savor His creation.

Job knew the wisdom found in nature. He told his friends:

> *Ask the animals, and they will instruct you; ask the birds of the sky, and they will tell you. Or speak to the earth, and it will instruct you; let the fish of the sea inform you. Which of all these does not know that the hand of the LORD has done this? The life of every living thing is in His hand, as well as the breath of all mankind.* (Job 12:7–10 HCSB)

When we take the time to look at a leaf, to touch its surface, to twirl its stem, we can be amazed at the intricacy of each delicate vein and blade God has made. When we lie back upon the grass, smell the dust from whence we were formed, feel the coolness of the soil beneath us, our eyes are drawn to the heavens above, the clouds and their various formations, the brightness of the sun, and we can't help but feel awe for the God who created all this beauty.

The psalmist says the trees in the forest sing for joy (Psalm 96:12). And if heaven and earth and everything in the sea are glad in Him and rejoice in Him (Psalm 69:34), why shouldn't we? When we consider how small we are compared to this universe, how grand the sun, moon, and stars He has created, we might wonder why He is mindful of us (Psalm 8:3–4). And then we remember Jesus' words, "You are even more precious to Him than a beautiful bird. If He looks after them, of course He will look after you" (Matthew 6:26 VOICE), and our worries take flight.

Today, find a way to get close to nature. Meditate on God's wonders (Psalm 145:5) and grow closer than ever to the Creator.

Lord, please speak to me as I draw closer to You amid Your glorious wonders.

Day 99

STRENGTH FOR THE DAY

My life dissolves and weeps itself away for heaviness; raise me up and strengthen me according to [the promises of] Your word. . . . My flesh and my heart may fail, but God is the Rock and firm Strength of my heart and my Portion forever.
PSALM 119:28; 73:26 AMPC

The troubles in this world are many. But thank the Lord we have a faithful God who hears our prayers. In those moments when you're so low you feel there's no way to go but up, go up. Raise your eyes to the heavens, and pray to the God who resides there as well as within you. Ask Him to strengthen you in and through His Word.

Throughout the Bible, God's people plead for His strength. While you may grow weak and weary as you walk His way, the God whose power no foe can withstand is there for you to give you all the strength you need to meet the challenges of the day before you.

Once you open yourself up to God, once you seek Him in His Word, you will soon be saying to yourself, "I have strength for all things in Christ Who empowers me [I am ready for anything and equal to anything through Him Who infuses inner strength]" (Philippians 4:13 AMPC).

God longs to be your strength every morning and to save you in times of trouble (Isaiah 33:2). And Jesus promised that with Him, you can do anything He calls you to do (Matthew 19:26). Because you walk in step with Him, you'll find courage as well as strength (Deuteronomy 31:6).

Your efforts are so tied in with the power He provides that you are encouraged to "seek the Lord and His strength; yearn for and seek His face and to be in His presence continually!" (1 Chronicles 16:11 AMPC).

Even when you are weak—*especially then*—you'll be strong because Jesus resides within you (2 Corinthians 12:9–10).

Today and every day, trust in God and be not afraid, for He is your strength, your song, and your Savior (Isaiah 12:2).

My Lord, when "my strength is gone, and I can hardly catch my breath. . . give me strength so I can stand according to Your word" [Daniel 10:17; Psalm 119:28 VOICE], so that I may walk in Your will and way.

Day 100

FOOD FOR THE ENTIRE YOU

Fill your minds with beauty and truth. Meditate on whatever is honorable, whatever is right, whatever is pure, whatever is lovely, whatever is good, whatever is virtuous and praiseworthy.
PHILIPPIANS 4:8 VOICE

When we meditate on God's truths and sink our minds into His Word, our entire being benefits. The promises God has made, the assurances He provides, the wonders He proclaims are food for our spirits and souls.

Many scripture verses calm our mind and body. Others arm us with strength, empower us to do what He calls us to do, or give us the patience to wait on Him. The apostle Paul, most likely penning Philippians while imprisoned, knew very well the effect God's Word had on his person.

One way to write God's Word upon your heart and mind or lay it up in your soul is not just to ponder or meditate on it but to memorize it. Then, in the most difficult of circumstances, you'll have a treasure trove of powerful, God-breathed words to draw upon. One way to start this armor-building habit is to dedicate yourself to memorizing one verse per week.

Here's a list of some of the most powerful Bible verses that will transform you from fearful to courageous, disheartened to hope filled, angry to self-controlled, sleepless to refreshed. Once you have these down, make up a list of your own verses to memorize, ones that especially touch your heart, buoy your spirit, and dispel worry, hurt, fear, or sorrow.

- "Don't worry; all will be well" (2 Kings 4:23 VOICE).
- "Be still, be calm, see, and understand I am the True God" (Psalm 46:10 VOICE).

- "Come to me, all of you who are weary and carry heavy burdens, and I will give you rest" (Matthew 11:28 NLT).
- "In peace I will lie down and sleep, for you alone, O LORD, will keep me safe" (Psalm 4:8 NLT).
- "His left hand cradles my head; his right embraces me" (Song of Solomon 2:6 VOICE).
- "Do not fear, for I am with you; do not be afraid, for I am your God. I will strengthen you; I will help you; I will hold on to you" (Isaiah 41:10 HCSB).
- "The LORD is close to the brokenhearted" (Psalm 34:18 NLT).
- "You will keep in perfect peace all who trust in you, all whose thoughts are fixed on you!" (Isaiah 26:3 NLT).
- "The LORD is my shepherd; there is nothing I lack" (Psalm 23:1 HCSB).

Lord, help me make Your Word a part of my heart, mind, spirit, and soul.

SCRIPTURE INDEX

Old Testament

New Testament